FLORI
TRE

By L. Frank Hudson
Cover Art and Illustrations by Mark Buzek

Published by Winner Enterprises

Editing by Lisa Braun-Kenigsberg
Cover and Illustrations by Mark Buzek
Design by George Hardy

A special thanks to Charlie's Locker, Ft. Lauderdale, Fla.

Maps: U.S. Department of Commerce, National Oceanic and Atmospheric Administration, National Ocean Service

International Standard Book Number 0-932855-29-6
Library of Congress Catalog Card Number 85—82086
Printed and bound in the United States of America

NOTE: Locations of treasure sites are speculative. Winner Enterprises takes no responsibility for correctness of sites.
Charts are NOT to be used for navigation.

Introduction

The purpose of this book is to provide information about Florida shipwrecks so that divers and amateur archaeologists may know what treasures lie hidden beneath the water's surface.

While space does not allow for listing every sunken ship off the Florida coast, I have attempted to include as many as possible.

I have gathered information about these sites from many sources including the Archives of the Indies in Seville, Spain; the Public Records Office in London; the Royal Dutch Archives in The Hague; the Vatican Library in Rome; the United States National Archives in Washington, D.C.; and from personal experience and many friends and acquaintances.

The period I investigated covers the 16th to the 20th centuries. While doing my research, I found the archivists to be most helpful. Without their help this book would not have been possible.

In the pages that follow, you will find a variety of sites, along with a selection of maps showing their approximate locations. The research of many years lie within these pages and with a little effort, treasure hunters of all kinds may share in the excitement and intrigue of the search for sunken treasure.

L. Frank Hudson

Letter To A Treasure Seeker

Dear Friend,

I have spent nearly 38 years doing factual research on treasure sites in the many Archives of the world. My advice to you, dear friend, is that there are three major factors involved in your search — good research, good equipment and adequate financing of your venture.

In doing your own research, I suggest that you begin with your local libraries. After you have exhausted those resources, continue to your local and state Archives. Other excellent sources, if you have the funds, are the National Archives in Washington, D.C., the Navy Department and the Department of Commerce. Also, be sure to consult the various publications having to do with treasure sources.

Now that you have sifted through the information, don't just rush to the site, expecting to become rich overnight. Wait until you have adequate time to stay and do it right. And be sure to budget for good equipment, as the tools for your discovery must be sufficient and appropriate. I know of too many cases where a group has traveled to a site without allowing enough time, and had to return home to their jobs, leaving an open hole for someone else to find and make the recovery. Whether hunting the land or the sea, leave enough time.

Now, try not to get discouraged. I know of one land site where a cofferdam (a watertight enclosure built to expose the bottom so that construction may be undertaken) was built by a group from Tampa on the Peach River. They spent a lot of money constructing it, going down 14 feet with a heavy pump. At that level they hit a log and simply quit, instead of finding if anything was under the log. Another man that I knew, who knew about the operation waited for them to pack up and leave. Then he pumped out the hole that had filled with water and built an "A" frame over it and got the log out with a chain hoist. And there was the chest sitting there. It had been under the log all the time. He got it out and has never worked a day since.

In sum, my friend, good research, good equipment and adequate financing are important in your quest. But more than anything, perseverence is the quality that will be most valuable to you in your search for treasure.

Happy hunting!

History Amid The Glitter

MEL FISHER'S FABULOUS FIND

On July 20, 1985 a 16-year-search for the Spanish galleon *Nuestra Senora de Atocha* was brought to an end with seven words from Kane Fisher, son of master treasure hunter, Mel Fisher. The words, "Put away the charts, I've found it!" were music to the ears of Mel Fisher and his determined company, Treasure Salvors, Inc. The three-century rest of the Atocha was over.

It is estimated that over $300 million in bounty was discovered from the galleon, her gold bars still shimmering as they did centuries ago. The mound of gold, silver and hull structure measured 100 feet long by 60 feet wide and about 5 feet in depth. On one day alone, the largest amount of gold salvaged from a treasure ship was removed from the wreck. And to date Fisher's divers have unearthed gold, emeralds, and priceless artifacts. More than 900 silver bars were found, many weighing 70 pounds or more.

The anchor of the wreck was discovered in approximately 20 feet of water just west of the Marquesas, the uninhabited mangrove islands that lie 35 miles west of Key West. The location of the anchor proved to be just seven miles northwest of where the Atocha went down. Her hull and cargo lie at the reef's outer edge in approximately 53 feet of water. Quite a ways off from the projected sinking of the galleon!

On many occasions Mel Fisher has been compared to an entrepreneur named Melian who was commissioned by King Phillip IV to run a salvage mission in the year 1625 to find the sunken galleon Atocha. The ship had been carrying South American silver that was brought aboard at the Isthmus of Panama along with gold from Cartagena. It had been en route to Spain to replenish the palace treasures. The king was adamant that the cargo be salvaged. Records from the Spanish archives show that Melian's attempt was the only successful one, except that the booty recovered was not actually from the Atocha, but from her sister vessel, the Santa Margarita. By using a bronze diving bell Melian and his group recovered some of her treasures, but nothing near in comparison to the "Fisher Find."

Much like the inventive Melian, Mel Fisher's ingenuity and

perseverance were crucial to his success. Years of struggle — a battle over salvage rights settled by the Supreme Court in the treasure hunters' favor — and tragedy — the loss of family when one of their vessels capsized — were a few of the many obstacles Fisher and his "believers" overcame in their quest for sunken treasure.

The Atocha's hull, half of which is still intact, is one of the earliest examples of shipbuilding. Since she was built in 1618, three decades after the Armada was destroyed at the hands of the British, the Atocha will most probably provide clues to the state-of-the-art of Spanish shipbuilding, among other valuable clues to that period of life at that time in history.

It is doubtless that Mel Fisher or any of his group will ever put all *their* charts away. There are too many ships still to be found.

INDIAN KEY, THE WRECKERS' RENDEZVOUS.

Florida's East Coast

Southeastern Florida: The Keys

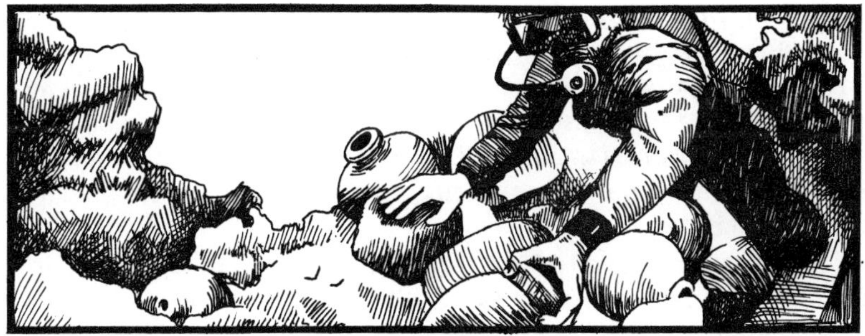

These small islands, called Keys or cays by the Spanish, form a chain now linked by the Overseas Highway from Key Largo curving southwest to Key West, the southernmost city in the continental United States.

The Keys, surrounded by treacherous but beautiful reefs, is the home of hundreds of shipwrecks from several centuries. Not only were the reefs deadly, even for the most skillful sailors, but frequent hurricanes took their toll as well.

For 400 years, the Spanish fleet sailed annually from Florida's east coast and Havana, Cuba — just 90 miles south of Key West — back to Spain. Most of the wrecks off the Keys are of Spanish origin. The most famous — and justifiably so — is the 350-year-old galleon Nuestra Senora de Atocha, whose treasure was finally uncovered in the summer of 1985 after 16 years of searching by professional treasure hunter Mel Fisher. The gold, silver and gems Fisher and his crew discovered is estimated to be worth over 300 million and will take at least two years to bring the total "find" to the surface.

In many cases, thc wrecks have become covered with sand, which must first be removed before the actual recovery can begin. However, the first step is to locate the site of the wreck.

While every effort has been made to pinpoint each shipwreck as accurately as possible on the maps, tides, currents and winds may have caused some locations to shift. But in looking for one site, you may stumble on another — perhaps one that had never been documented. The search goes on.

SITE #1

WRECK OF THE "ARAUCANA" (1811)

The Araucana was a small Spanish warship with 10 guns under the command of Capt. Benito de la Rigada of the Royal Spanish Navy. She regularly carried the mails from Havana to Cadiz, Spain, along with some supplies. On her return trip, she carried weapons of war.

The Araucana left Havana on a clear, bright October day in 1811 and had an uneventful crossing of the Florida Strait. But as the second day approached, heavy rain clouds could be seen ahead and before evening, the ship encountered strong squalls that grew to hurricane force before morning. By the third morning, the Araucana was in the midst of a full-blown hurricane which broke her main mast in two places and fell to the deck, tearing a hole in the hull. The crew managed to escape drowning by climbing into the lifeboats, which had been fitted with provisions when the weather turned ominous. Within only moments after the crew left the ship, she took a nosedive and sank about a half mile from the middle of Eliott Key in almost 75 feet of water. The crew got to shore and camped there until a passing ship took them to Nassau, where they hitched a ride to Havana.

The Araucana is said to have carried hundreds of thousands of dollars in coins from the Spanish royal treasury, all of which went down with the ship.

SITE #2

TWO SPANISH GALLEONS (1689)

Two galleons, each carrying a million dollars in gold and silver from the Spanish fleet, sank off the northern end of Key Largo during a storm. The Archives of the Indies in Spain did not identify the ships but did state that they sank at this location. These ships are certainly worth finding.

SITE #3

SPANISH GALLEON (1689)
"NUESTRA SENORE CONCEPTION Y SAN JOSEFE" (1689)

This ship is another member of the 1689 fleet which was caught in a hurricane and sank on its way to Spain with treasures from the New World. She should be a very rich find. No map site.

SITE #4

SPANISH GALLEON "EL CAPITANA EL RUBI" (1733)

El Capitana el Rubi carried 60 cannons and about $5 million in gold coins and silver artifacts. She sank off the southern end of Key Largo in more than 100 feet of water. The crew was saved but the treasure lost.

SITE #5

SPANISH GALLEON "SANTA MARGARITA" (1622)

The Santa Margarita was carrying about a million dollars in gold and silver when she sank in 30 feet of water off Matecumbe Key. This sister vessel went down in the same storm as the Atocha. According to records found by Eugene Lyon of the University of Florida in a Seville archive, an entrepreneur named Melian was sent by King Philip IV to find the sister ship Nuestra Senora de Atocha, but found some of the Santa Margarita treasure in 1625. Although some has been found there is much treasure still to be located.

SITE #6

FIVE SPANISH GALLEONS (1622)

The vessels, part of the royal fleet that sank during a hurricane in 1622, went down off Lower Matecumbe Key. Each was known to have been carrying at least one million dollars in gold and silver, and each would make a rich find. No map site.

SITE #7

BRITISH MERCHANT SHIP "EVENLY" (1803)

The Evenly was sailing from Jamaica to Liverpool, England, with a cargo of raw sugar. During a storm she took on water and began to sink. Her captain managed to beach her and had the ship's chest buried on shore. The crew was able to salvage enough timbers to build rudimentary shelters where they lived until a passing British ship rescued them. A later hurricane blew the Evenly back into the sea where she sank in deeper waters. No map site.

SITE #8

UNIDENTIFIED WRECK

An unidentified shipwreck lies in about 120 feet of water on the ocean side of Grassy Key. She is not likely to have been a royal galleon since she did not carry many cannons. She was possibly a Spanish merchant ship, though some silver wedge bars were found on her by divers.

SITE #9

UNIDENTIFIED WRECK

This shipwreck is found just offshore the south end of Sandy Point on Coco Plum Key. She is believed to have been a three-masted sailing schooner about 110 to 120 feet long, 25 to 30 feet in beam (wide) with a draft (depth) of seven to 12 feet. She probably had three decks. Judging from the available information, this wreck is likely to have been a British ship transporting raw sugar from the Caribbean to England in the early 1800's. Her ship's chest is said to be intact. No map site.

SITE #10

UNKNOWN GALLEON AT VACA KEY

A galleon of unknown heritage lies on the north end of Vaca Key. Divers have found gold coins on her. She may be worth exploring.

SITE #11

UNIDENTIFIED WRECK

This shipwreck lies just off the southwestern side of Knight Key in fairly shallow water. She may have been a schooner, about 90 feet long. Nothing is known of her origin or cargo.

SITE #12

UNIDENTIFIED WRECK

A second wreck is located near Site No. 11, off the Atlantic side of Knight Key. From her size, she could have been a galleon, judging from the cannons seen by divers.

SITE #13

UNIDENTIFIED WRECK

Located on the Atlantic side of Big Pine Key, this shipwreck may have been from the Spanish fleet that used to sail from Havana, Cuba, to Spain. At various times it is covered and uncovered with sand, depending on the currents.

SITE #14

UNIDENTIFIED WRECK

This shipwreck is believed to have been a Spanish galleon loaded with silver bars that sank in the late 1600's. It lies under about 10 feet of sand in Sacarme Bay at Summerland Key.

According to the Jamaican Archives in Spanishtown, Jamaica, the ship — whose name is not in the records — was headed back to Spain from Veracruz, Mexico with a cargo of silver. She became separated from the fleet during a storm and was later threatened by pirates whose leader gave orders to board the galleon. Instead, the captain of the galleon quickly gave orders to beach the ship. His crew obediently ran her aground on a nearby sandbar. The Spanish captain and crew then went ashore and hid in the bushes while the pirates boarded the galleon and took what they wanted. After the thieves left, the Spaniards returned to the ship and took enough provisions to sail on to Jamaica in their lifeboats.

SITE #15

UNIDENTIFIED WRECK

Located near the mouth of Sugarloaf Creek on the Atlantic side of Sugarloaf Key, this wreck is thought to have been a schooner not more than 60 feet in length. Compared to other ships of the time, she was not very big but good things have been known to be found in small packages.

SITE #16

BRITISH FRIGATE H.M.S. "LOOE" (1744)

On February 5, 1744, the British frigate H.M.S. Looe sank during a severe storm in about 70 feet of water off a small island that has since washed away. The wreckage lies about a half mile off the northern end of Bahia Honda Key.

SITE #17

SPANISH MERCHANT SHIP "SAN ANTONIO" (1768)

The San Antonio was on her way from Havana to Cadiz, Spain, with a load of coins, tobacco and other goods as well as some passengers. She ran into a hurricane just off the present day city of Key West where she sank. All the passengers and crew were saved but the cargo was lost. The San Antonio may prove to be a rich find for a lucky treasure hunter.

SITE #18

SPANISH GALLEON "NUESTRA SENORA DE ATOCHA" (1622)

Nuestra Senora de Atocha, made famous by treasure hunter Mel Fisher who uncovered her "mother lode" worth over $300 million, sank 40 miles west of Key West during the 1622 hurricane that destroyed the Spanish fleet.

The Atocha was built in Havana in 1620 to service the royal flotilla on its homeward journey by supplying men and materials for shipboard repairs on the way to Spain. But for a reason we do not know, in 1622 the Atocha became a full-fledged member of the fleet, carrying a king's fortune. On July 20, 1985 her treasures were once again seen and marveled at by human eyes. **The Atocha has been found and is without a doubt the largest ever discovered in history.**

SITE #19

SPANISH SCHOONER AT DRY TORTUGAS

Several miles west off Garden Key is an old wreck with six brass cannons which according to a diver who has seen the site is of Spanish origin. She was about 90 feet long and is believed to have been sunk by pirates.

SITE #20

DUTCH WARSHIP

Just north of the Dry Tortugas is a wreck believed to be a Dutch warship sunk in the early 1800's by pirates.

SITE #21

BRITISH SHIP "GRENVILLE PACKET" (1765)

The Grenville Packet washed up on the beach at Garden Key in May, 1765, during a hurricane. Her passengers and crew took refuge on the beach and later built crude shelters from the ship's timbers. Sometime later, they were rescued and taken to St. Augustine, which was British territory at the time. The ship's strongbox was not recovered.

Southeastern Florida: Biscayne Bay

Biscayne Bay is an inlet of the Atlantic Ocean which separates Miami from Miami Beach. Its most famous island is Key Biscayne, where former President Richard Nixon had his winter White House.

SITE #22

H.M.S. "SEA WOLF" (1780)

The H.M.S. Sea Wolf was a British frigate armed with 10 cannons. She had been in a fight with a French pirate ship off the coast of the Dry Tortugas, which were known to be a pirate stronghold, where she became badly shot up. The Sea Wolf was limping toward more civilized St. Augustine when a hurricane ran her into a treacherous reef in Biscayne Bay, causing her to sink. No map site.

SITE #23

UNKNOWN SPANISH GALLEON

This unknown Spanish galleon is believed to have sunk during the mid 1600s, judging from the dates inscribed on her cannons. Some gold and silver coins have already been found at the site; more may await the treasure seeker. No map site.

SITE #24

SPANISH GALLEON "SANTA MARGARITA"

While there have been reports of three other locations where the Santa Margarita went down, research at the Archives of the Indies in Seville, Spain, discloses that the galleon sank in fairly shallow water in lower Biscayne Bay. As she was wrecked with more than $7 million in gold in her hold, the Santa Margarita is certainly worth finding. A wide area to search. No map site.

SITE #25

TWO UNIDENTIFIED SHIPS

The remains of two unidentified ships lie to the east of the old Biscayne Bay lighthouse, in about 40 feet of water. While nothing is known about their history, they are presumed to be Spanish vessels and the artifacts found near the site appear to be of Spanish origin.

SITE #26

BRITISH SHIP H.M.S. "WINCHESTER" (1695)

The Winchester was a British warship sailing from Jamaica to London when she came too close to a reef and tore a jagged hole in her side. Realizing the ship was going down, her crew manned the lifeboats which had been outfitted with fresh water and food. From the safety of these small boats, they watched their ship sink to the bottom before setting sail for Jamaica, where the men arrived 46 days later. No map site.

SITE #27

BRITISH SHIP "HOWLETT" (1744)

The Howlett was lost just southeast of Cape Florida on Key Biscayne where she struck a reef. The crew was saved but her cargo — which consisted entirely of gold dust and coins — was declared a total loss by Lloyds of London, which had insured the ship.

SITE #28

UNKNOWN GALLEON WRECK

Another galleon wreck lies southeast of the historic Cape Florida lighthouse located in what is now Bill Baggs Cape Florida State Recreation Area on the southern end of Key Biscayne.

SITE #29

BRITISH SHIP "GENERAL CONWAY" (1763)

The General Conway was on her way from Kingston, Jamaica, to London when she hit a reef during a hurricane. She sank about a half mile east of the Gulf Stream off the southern tip of Key Biscayne. The passengers and crew were saved; her cargo, which contained a number of silver bars, was not.

SITE #30

BRITISH SHIP H.M.S. "TYGER" (1742)

The Tyger, a British warship, was chasing a pirate ship when she ran onto a reef. Seeing that their situation was hopeless, the Tyger's captain gave orders to abandon ship after stowing a supply of fresh water and food in the lifeboats. The crew rowed to a sand key, or small island, where they lived for some months until they were finally rescued by a passing ship. No map site.

Notes

Florida's Central Atlantic Coast

This area covers shipwreck sites from Ormond Beach, just north of popular Daytona Beach, to Jupiter, which lies between Ft. Pierce to the north and Palm Beach to the south. This stretch of the Atlantic includes some of the best known Spanish wrecks in Florida.

SITE #31

WRECK OF THE "DOVE" (1733)

The English slave ship Dove floundered just offshore from Ormond Beach during a hurricane in the fall of 1773. She was carrying 100 slaves from the west coast of Africa to Savannah, Georgia. Of the 100 slaves onboard, 80 drowned along with the ship's captain and two crew members. The remaining 20 slaves were taken ashore with their iron shackles and chains, in lifeboats. The Africans, though saved from drowning, could not be rescued from bondage and were later sold at the slave market in St. Augustine.

The Dove finally sank about three-quarters of a mile offshore from Ormond Beach. Her strongbox is worth discovering.

SITE #32

UNIDENTIFIED WRECK

An unidentified wreck lies just inside Ponce de Leon inlet, north of New Smyrna Beach. It is believed to have been a Spanish ship, sunk during a hurricane.

SITE #33

SPANISH SHIP "PEDRO MENENDEZ" (1572)

A spanish cargo ship, the Pedro Menendez went down during a hurricane in 1572 about a mile offshore from what is now Cape Canaveral. In her hold were gold Spanish coins which were a great loss to the Spaniards of the area.

SITE #34

SPANISH GALLEON, POSSIBLY THE "SAN PEDRO"(1597)

A Spanish galleon believed to be the San Pedro was carrying over a million dollars in gold when she sank in 1597 about a mile offshore to the east of Cape Canaveral.

The ship was part of the annual fleet that sailed from Veracruz, Mexico, to Havana and on to Spain. The Spanish fleet was sailing northward along the eastern coast of Florida when a hurricane struck. The San Pedro lost her masts, which fell with such impact that they tore a hole in her side. Most of the crew made it to shore where they lived on the fish and game they could catch until a passing Spanish ship rescued them and took them to Havana.

SITE #35

BRITISH SHIP "H.M.S. WOLFF" (1741)

Located just offshore from Cocoa Beach — a few miles south of Cape Canaveral — is the wreckage of the British warship H.M.S. Wolff, which got caught in a hurricane and sank. She carried 26 guns, most of which were bronze. The ship was sailing from Kingston, Jamaica, to New York. Many lives were lost in the wreck.

SITE #36

UNIDENTIFIED SPANISH GALLEONS (1715)

The main ships of the 1715 Spanish fleet were washed ashore and sank. Two of the wrecks are on the south side of one of the inlets. But since both sites are leased by a private company from the state of Florida, the Green Cabin wreck and the Anchor wreck (as they have come to be called) are presently out of bounds to any other treasure hunters. No map site.

SITE #37

BRITISH SCHOONER "BETSEY" (1788)

The British schooner Betsey sank during a hurricane in September 1788 while carrying cargo from Liverpool, England, to Pensacola, Florida, where she was due to pick up a cargo of lumber and hides for the return voyage. She lost her masts during the storm and the currents carried her into Vero Beach, where a second storm sank her. The ship's chest went down with her.

SITE #38

THREE SPANISH GALLEONS (1565)

Three unidentified Spanish galleons are known to have sunk in 1565 just north of present day Ft. Pierce. They were part of a fleet sailing from Havana to St. Augustine when they ran aground on the beach during a storm. All three ships were carrying soldiers and supplies as well as payroll for the troops at the St. Augustine fort.

The crews were able to build crude shelters on shore made of the ships' timbers and they salvaged a sufficient amount of food to survive until they were rescued by a ship sailing south to Havana.

SITE #39

THE GOLD WEDGE WRECK UNIDENTIFIED SPANISH WRECK

The site is located just north of Ft. Pierce and is commonly called the Gold Wedge Wreck. The Spanish packed gold wedges into a circle inside clay crocks sealed with wooden plugs. They could then be rolled on and off the ships using long planks placed between the shore and the ship's deck. Once the gold wedges arrived in Spain they were melted down at the royal mint and either made into coins or rectangular gold bars.

SITE #40

BRITISH BARK "NANTWICH" (1696)

The British ship Nantwich was carrying $10,000 in gold when she sank just south of Ft. Pierce on October 10, 1696, during a hurricane. She had been en route from Jamaica to London with a cargo of raw sugar. While the crew escaped to shore, she was considered a total loss by her owners.

If the wreck was located and the gold coins recovered from her strong box, they would be very valuable as artifacts.

SITE #41

BRITISH SHIP "BURROUGH" (1696)

The Burrough was probably sunk by the same hurricane that sank the Nantwich. She was sailing from London to Jamaica with $5000 in gold coins in her strongbox to purchase cargo for her return voyage. She was dismasted by the storm, which blew her up on the rocks at a Jupiter lighthouse where she broke up and sank. The chest of gold went down with her.

SITE #42

BRITISH BARKENTINE "REFORMATION" (1696)

The Reformation, an elaborately rigged three-masted vessel, was sailing from Liverpool to New Orleans with a load of hardware. In July 1696, a storm drove her ashore just north of Jupiter inlet. The crew escaped to shore in the lifeboat, where they waited until the storm passed and then returned to the wreck to salvage enough material to rig a sail to get them to Jamaica. They were able to gather enough salt pork and biscuits from the ship, combined with fresh water from a nearby spring which they used to fill their water casks, to complete the abbreviated journey. Documents show that the industrious crew also salvaged the Reformation's strongbox.

SITE #43

UNKNOWN SPANISH GALLEON

An unknown Spanish galleon wreck lies in fairly shallow water to the south of the Jupiter inlet. It is understood that she lies in 6 fathoms of water.

Northeastern Florida: St. Augustine

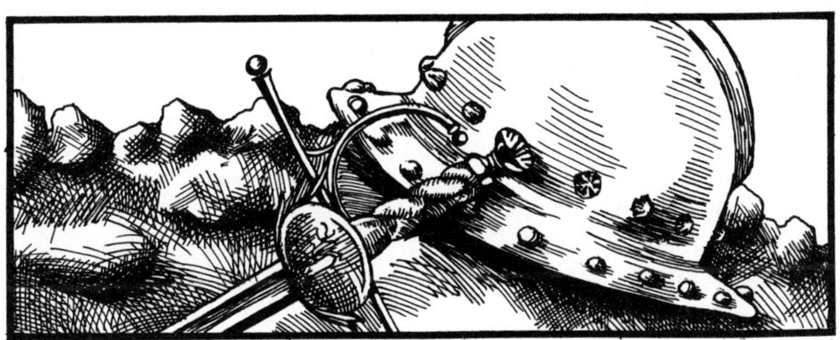

The sandbar at St. Augustine spelled the destruction of many of the ships that tried to sail into its harbor between the 16th and 19th centuries. Lacking modern dredging methods, the ships had to cut a path through the treacherous sandbar at high tide, hoping to get safely across. Many failed in the attempt and ran aground. Stuck in the sand, the ships broke up and were abandoned to tides and time.

St. Augustine is the nation's oldest city, said to have first been claimed by Ponce de Leon in 1513 who took possession for Spain. The first permanent European settlement in what became the United States was established here in 1565 by Spanish admiral Don Pedro Menendez de Aviles.

SITE #44

RUSSIAN FRIGATE "JULIANA" (1817)

The Juliana was sailing from St. Ubes, Portugal, to the port of Savannah, Georgia, when she was blown off course. She washed ashore three miles south of the St. Augustine lighthouse in September, 1817. The ship's cargo consisted of rope, olive oil, cork, wine and other goods. Her strongbox contained some $6000 in gold and silver rubles.

SITE #45

SCHOONER AMERICAN COIN (1853)

The American Coin was sailing from Savannah, Georgia, bound for St. Augustine when she sprang a leak. The crew manned the pumps and managed to keep her afloat until they approached the city. There she was beached near the lighthouse on Anastasia Island where the crew members were able to swim ashore. The wreck itself gradually settled and was covered by sand.

The American Coin's strongbox is still buried with her. Also, her heavy lead keel should bring a good price from a scrap metal dealer.

SITE #46

AMERICAN SCHOONER "VENUS" (1842)

The Venus was carrying a cargo of granite building blocks from Maine to St. Augustine. The ship had almost arrived at her destination when she was caught in a violent hurricane and ran aground between the St. Augustine lighthouse and a sandbar. All the crew members were saved.

The weight of the ship's heavy cargo caused her to sink into the sand faster than usual and there she rests today.

SITE #47

AMERICAN PRIVATEER "JEFFERSON DAVIS" (1861)

A small brig (a two-masted vessel square-rigged on both masts), the Jefferson Davis was a privateer, meaning it operated under a license known as a Letter of Marque from the Confederate Congress which permitted the ship to capture of harass the North's merchant ships.

In the summer of 1861, while being chased by a Union warship, the Jeff Davis tried to escape to the safety of the port of St. Augustine. There she hit a sandbar and stuck fast. Her hull split open and she began sinking. Meanwhile, shells from the U.S. warship set the privateer afire and she burned to the water line before being completely submerged.

Though the crew escaped in lifeboats, the Jeff Davis' strongbox containing $11,000 in U.S. minted gold coins still remains aboard. Her heavy lead keel may also be worth salvaging for scrap metal.

SITE #48

BRITISH SCHOONER "THE HAMBRO SHIP" (1817)

The Hambro Ship was carrying a cargo of raw sugar from Kingston, Jamaica to England when she was caught in a hurricane which dismasted her. The schooner ran aground on Anastasia Island about 12 miles south of the lighthouse. Her crew was saved but the strongbox went down with the ship. It is said to have contained 8000 English gold sovereigns, once equal to one pound sterling apiece and now worth many times their face value today.

SITE #49

UNNAMED SPANISH SHIPS IN ST. AUGUSTINE HARBOR (1803)

Eight Spanish ships sank in St. Augustine Harbor during a hurricane in 1803. The Spanish Archives lists them as a group, not giving individual information. However, one was carrying the payroll for the soldiers stationed in the St. Augustine fort. Several of the ships were said to belong to the King of Spain and were carrying gold and silver coins from Veracruz, Mexico, to Spain. The remaining vessels were merchant ships.

SITE #50

AMERICAN SCHOONER "TWO SISTERS" (1822)

In September 1822, the Two Sisters was on her way from New Orleans to Boston with a load of cotton. Hit by a hurricane, the ship was driven up on the beach about 10 miles from the lighthouse on Anastasia Island. A second hurricane pushed the ship back into the water where she sank to a depth of 43 feet.

The Two Sister's strongbox and heavy lead keel are worth salvaging.

SITE #51

SCHOONER "AMERICAN FROLIC" (1816)

The American Frolic was sailing from New York to New Orleans when a hurricane blew her ashore about five miles south of the lighthouse on Anastasia Island. The schooner is said to have been carrying a considerable amount of money in her strongbox for trading purposes, mostly in gold coins.

SITE #52

PORTUGUESE BARK "EDWARDO THE FIRST" (1828)

This three-masted ship was sailing from Rio de Janeiro, Brazil, to Portugal and carried the royal mail, coins and uncut diamonds as well as a dozen or so passengers. A severe storm drove the ship onto shore about three miles due south of the present lighthouse. Her passengers and crew were all saved but some gold bars and her strongbox were not recovered. A second storm followed and blew the wreck back into about 50 feet of water where she sank.

SITE #52A

UNNAMED SPANISH SHIP (1626)

In 1626, a ship carrying the pay for the soldiers in St. Augustine fort arrived from Veracruz, Mexico, and ran aground on the sandbar at the harbor's entrance. The ship's hull tore open and she sank. The entire crew escaped in lifeboats but the ship sank too quickly into the deep water at the end of the sandbar for any of the payroll to be saved.

The ship carried about $8000 in pieces of eight (Spanish silver coins) along with four bronze cannons, four iron cannons, a quantity of cannon balls, and 30 muskets.

SITE #53

ENGLISH SCHOONER "NEW PLYMOUTH" (1833)

The New Plymouth was a three-masted schooner on her way from Liverpool, England, to New Orleans with a cargo of rope, whiskey, foodstuffs, hardware, and other merchandise. She also carried a considerable amount of gold sovereigns in her strongbox for the purchases of cotton, hides and other products of the Mississippi Valley area.

The New Plymouth sailed into the St. Augustine harbor with high winds behind her. The ship struck the deadly sandbar and sank. The crew and some of the cargo were saved but her gold-filled strongbox went down with the ship.

SITE #54

SPANISH SHIP "SANTO CHRISTO DE MARCIBO" (1706)

The Santa Christo de Marcibo was part of the Spanish fleet returning to Spain in 1706. She had left Havana, Cuba, in September of that year when the ship sailed into a hurricane north of Melbourne, Florida, near present day Cape Canaveral. Her masts were destroyed and she was blown northward. The Santo Christo de Marcibo finally sank in deep water about 24 miles southeast of St. Augustine. The ship and its entire cargo of gold and silver was declared a total loss by the trading firm that operated her out of Seville, Spain.

SITE #55

ENGLISH SHIP "WHITE SWAN" (1803)

The White Swan was sailing from Plymouth, England to Savannah, Georgia, with a cargo of tea, cloth, iron, hardware and other goods as well as several passengers. Her first port of call before Savannah was St. Augustine, where she sank while trying to navigate the treacherous sandbar in the harbor's mouth. The passengers were all saved but the cargo and strongbox were lost.

SITE #56

ENGLISH SHIP "EAST FLORIDA MERCHANT" (1733)

The East Florida Merchant sank trying to cross the St. Augustine sandbar during a bad storm. She went down with $8000 in gold coins in her strongbox, which is worth considerably more today.

SITE #57

SHIP AT MATANZAS INLET (1632)

This was a Spanish cargo vessel that sank in a hurricane and was dragged by the currents to the Matanzas Inlet where she was finally submerged in 18 feet of water. She was carrying gold bars and coins.

SITE #58

UNNAMED SPANISH SHIP (1627)

The ship was traveling from Veracruz, Mexico bound for St. Augustine with a payroll intended to replace that lost in an earlier shipwreck (see Site No. 52A). She carried 12,000 silver pesos along with four bronze and four iron cannons for protection. Sadly, the frigate met the same fate as the previous ship. The crew was saved but again, the cargo was lost. No map site.

A SPANISH TREASURE-FRIGATE

Notes

Northeastern Florida: Amelia Island

Amelia Island with its principal city of Fernandina Beach (formerly Fernandina) is home to hundreds of shipwrecked sailing ships blown in by hurricanes and storms over a 300-year period. Just how many ships are sunk here will probably never be known.

Amelia Island is 30 miles northeast of Jacksonville, adjacent to the Georgia border, on Florida's Atlantic coast.

SITE #59

WRECK OF THE "ALVAREZ" (1861)

Early in the morning of August 5, 1861, the townspeople of Fernandina awoke to the thunder of ships' guns. From the beach on the Atlantic side of Amelia Island, they witnessed a battle taking place about a mile and a half from shore between a Confederate privateer and the United States warship Hatteras. The privateer, named the Jefferson Davis, was a privately owned ship commissioned by the South to harass enemy ships in the area.

Caught in the battle was the Alvarez, which had been captured by the Jeff Davis off the Bahamas and was now being escorted by the Confederate ship to Charleston, S.C. The Alvarez had been sailing toward her home port of Boston from Capetown, South Africa, when she was seized by the Jeff Davis.

Realizing that they were in danger of capture themselves by the Hatteras, the Confederate crew manning the Alvarez ran her onto a sandbar. Before abandoning ship in lifeboats, they set her ablaze and then rowed to shore and safety.

The Alvarez gradually sank in the sandbar and today lies under six feet of sand about one and a half miles due east of the north end of Amelia Island. The ship's skin rotted away many years ago, but the scrap copper may be worth going after. Also, the ship is reported to still have its strongbox.

SITE #60

SWEDISH SHIP "NICHOLAS ADOLPH" (1818)

The Nicholas Adolph was on her way from Sweden to the West Indies to purchase raw sugar in the fall of 1818 when she was blown ashore by a severe hurricane. She later slid off the sandbar onto which the ship had floundered and sank in deeper water.

The Nicholas Adolph had been carrying a considerable number of coins in her strongbox. No map site.

SITE #61

BRITISH SHIP "BETSEY" (1812)

The Betsey was on her way to London from Jamaica with a cargo of raw sugar when she sank off the southern end of Amelia Island in 12 feet of water during a severe hurricane. She was carrying $10,000 worth of coins, which would be worth considerably more today.

SITE #62

SPANISH FRIGATE "SANTA BARBARA" (1765)

The Santa Barbara was lost in a hurricane, at the southern end of Amelia Island, while carrying supplies from Havana to Fort San Carlos at Fernandina. She is also said to have been carrying the payroll for 20 men.

SITE #63

UNKNOWN SPANISH GALLEON (1748)

She is believed to have been one of seven ships blown off course during a hurricane which separated them from the Spanish fleet traveling from Havana to Cadiz, Spain in 1748. It isn't certain which of the seven ships she was.

She lies just inside Nassau Sound.

SITE #64

Note: There are three small islands at the mouth of Nassau Sound where gold Spanish coins frequently wash ashore after a strong northeastern wind, indicating a wreck. It has yet to be found and identified.

Florida's West Coast

Southwestern Florida: The Everglades to Sarasota

In the Gulf of Mexico, off the coast of Everglades National Park to the south and the Florida Panhandle to the north, lie hundreds of shipwrecks of several nations and centuries. Pirates once roamed these waters and their stolen treasures lie at the bottom of many a harbor or inlet along the state's west coast. Hurricanes, too, took their deadly toll along with battles of the Civil War and World War II.

SITE #65

WRECK OF THE "RHEE GALLEY" (1774)

In July 1744, the British cargo ship Rhee Galley was on her way from Liverpool, England, to New Orleans when she sailed into a hurricane. The ship was blown off course into a shallow area off Cape Sable in what is now Everglades National Park, near the mouth of Ponce de Leon Bay. The Rhee Galley became stuck in the sand and had to be abandoned by her crew. Though most of her cargo was later recovered by another British ship, her strongbox was not and went down with the ship as she gradually sank in the sand.

SITE #66

UNKNOWN SPANISH WRECK (1760)

An unknown Spanish wreck lies just offshore at the entrance to Ponce de Leon Bay. A cannon recovered from the site several years ago bore the year 1760 and appeared to be of Spanish origin. No more is known about her.

SITE #67

WRECK AT LOSTMANS RIVER

Another wreck of unknown origin lies at the mouth of Lostmans River in what is now Everglades National Park. It is likely she was a ship from one of the Spanish fleets sailing from Mexico to Havana that became separated from the others in a storm and was later attacked by pirates, as frequently happened in these waters. After a ship was pillaged and the crew murdered, the pirates would scuttle her in the mouth of a shallow river and move on to their next target. This was common practice in the pirate world.

SITE #68

BRITISH SHIP "BELIZE" (1763)

The Belize was carrying cargo from Liverpool to Pensacola on Florida's panhandle when she was driven into the mouth of Cannon Bay north of Lostman's River in the Everglades. There she foundered on a sandbar. Her crew managed to save the ship's merchandise and strongbox but artifacts remain for discovery.

SITE #69

UNKNOWN WRECK AT CAXAMBAS PASS

Another unknown wreck lies buried under six feet of sand at the mouth of Caximba Pass south of Marco Island. The ship was probably Spanish and a likely victim of a pirate raid.

SITE #70

SPANISH GALLEON AT NAPLES (1733)

This unnamed galleon was part of the 1733 Spanish fleet sailing from Veracruz, Mexico, to Havana and carrying about a million dollars in gold coins. The fleet was hit by a hurricane, sinking this particular galleon. The crew members all escaped and were picked up by other ships in the fleet and taken to Cuba. A salvage boat sent from Havana rescued part of the ship's cargo before a second storm caused the wreck to shift and become covered with a layer of sand.

For years, gold doubloons have been washing up on the beach at Naples and are believed to be coming from this wreck.

SITE #71

SPANISH GALLEON AT CLAM PASS (1733)

The galleon, located just north of Naples Beach about a mile offshore, seems to have been the sister ship of the one located at Site No. 70. While it is known that the Spanish lost two ships in this area in 1733, neither of the ships' names have been discovered.

While a salvage crew sent from Havana recovered some property, it is likely much still remains. After a strong northwestern wind, gold coins have been found on the beach on the south side of the pass.

SITE #72

PIRATE WRECK OFF BLACK ISLAND (1803)

Occasionally pirates — who were legion along Florida's west coast at one time — did receive their just rewards. In the fall of 1803, a British warship posing as a merchant vessel was approached by a ship which suddenly hoisted the Jolly Roger (pirate flag) and demanded that the British ship surrender. Instead, the crew of the imposter cargo ship fired a broadside attack on the pirate ship which tried to make a run for safety. The British warship followed in hot pursuit and finally sank the pirate vessel about a half mile offshore.

The gang of pirates was believed to have been part of Bill Margoza's motley crew from Tampa Bay. The survivors of the shipwreck were captured and while proclaiming their innocence all the time, were taken to shore and hanged by the British from the limbs of nearby pine trees.

SITE #73

SPANISH WRECK AT PUNTA RASSA (1529)

This wreck is believed to have been one of Spanish explorer Hernando de Soto's supply ships, which during a storm sank at the mouth of the Caloosahatchee River. Her cargo included the payroll for the de Soto expedition, several small cannons, muskets, and ammunition. No map site.

SITE #74

SPANISH SHIP "SAN CRISTOFORO" (1641)

The San Cristoforo is located just offshore the northern end of Sanibel Island in shallow water. She was part of the Spanish fleet sailing between Veracruz, Mexico, and Havana which was caught in a hurricane in 1641. Documents in Spain show that the San Cristoforo was carrying over a million dollars in gold bars and coins when she went down.

SITE #75

UNIDENTIFIED WRECK

Another Spanish wreck lies about a mile offshore the northern end of Sanibel Island. Divers have found gold coins at the site and it is likely there are more to be discovered.

SITE #76

CONFEDERATE SHIP "MARY QUEEN" (1863)

The Mary Queen was believed to have been a Confederate blockade runner carrying a cargo of guns and ammunition to Tampa. From Tampa, the war material would be shipped overland to the Confederate forces fighting in Virginia.

In 1863, the Mary Queen was attempting to run the North's blockade along Florida's west coast. At a point about a mile offshore from the northern end of Captiva Island at Redfish Pass, she was sighted by the United States warship Hatteras. The warship fired one shot across her bow to announce her intention of searching the smaller ship. Instead, the feisty Mary Queen let loose all her cannons on the Hatteras which returned the fire and sank the Confederate ship.

Her crew was taken aboard the Hatteras as prisoners of war and brought to an internment camp in Key West, where the warship was stationed.

SITE #77

PIRATE SHIP OFF LA COSTA ISLAND (1817)

A British warship caught pirates pillaging a British merchant ship off the Dry Tortugas and fired a cannon ball across her bow. The pirate ship turned and fled north, with the warship in hot pursuit. The chase continued until both ships were off the northern end of Costa Island (also known as Cayo Costa and La Costa) in Charlotte Harbor west of Ft. Myers. The warship got close enough to fire a volley which made a direct hit on the pirate ship, causing her to sink about a mile offshore.

Some of the pirates escaped by jumping in the water and swimming ashore. The less lucky ones were caught by the British and hanged.

SITE #78

PIRATE SHIP "FLORIDA BLANCA" (1821)

In 1821, after the United States bought Florida from Spain, one of the new owner's first acts was the establishment of an anti-piracy fleet stationed at Key West whose mission was to clean out pirate's nests in the Gulf of Mexico. Shippers had become afraid to send their vessels into the Gulf for fear of capture by these thieves. Shipping had come to a standstill and the U.S. Navy had orders to do something about it.

The pirate Jose Gaspar, better known as Gasparilla, had reached the age of 68 and decided to retire from the business of piracy. He thought he would go to one of the Latin American countries and live the life of a retired country gentleman. With the rising power of the United States and its control of Florida, piracy no longer seemed an easy way to make a living.

For some days prior to their departure to South America, Gaspar and his men were busy digging up various caches of gold around Charlotte Harbor and Tampa Bay. The treasures were stashed in the hold of his flagship, the Florida Blanca.

On the day they were to leave, the lookout spotted a merchant ship about two miles offshore. Gaspar couldn't resist taking one more prize before retiring, so the heavily laden Florida Blanca set out to make its last capture.

Nearing his prey, Gaspar ordered the Jolly Roger hoisted. At the same time, the other ship suddenly ran up the Stars and Stripes and dropped the canvas covering her sides, revealing herself as a United States warship.

Gaspar and his old-fashioned cannons were no match for the warship, which was equipped with the latest naval guns that shot farther and straighter than anything the pirate had at his disposal. Most of his men were wounded or killed and he received a serious injury. Realizing that the jig was finally up and knowing that the U.S. Navy usually hanged pirates on the spot, Gaspar wrapped himself in a length of heavy anchor chain and jumped overboard. The old pirate had chosen suicide over execution.

The Florida Blanca, with more than $11 million on board, sank just to the north of the main entrance to Boca Grande Harbor off what is now — fittingly enough — Gasparilla Island.

SITE #79

SPANISH GALLEON AT GASPARILLA PASS

A Spanish wreck is found at the Gulf entrance to Big Gasparilla Pass, with Gasparilla Island to the south and Little Gasparilla to the north. Her history remains to be discovered, along with any artifacts.

SITE #79A

UNIDENTIFIED AMERICAN FRIGATE (1821)

According to documents in Washington, D.C., an unidentified American frigate lies near the Gulf entrance to Big Gasparilla Pass, at the northern end of Gasparilla Island. The frigate was said to have been carrying over a million dollars in coins when she was attacked by pirates, who sank her.

SITE #80

UNIDENTIFIED WRECK AT BOCILLA PASS (1817)

A cannon recovered from the site of a wreck at Bocilla Pass north of Little Gasparilla Island dates the ship from 1817. It is believed she was captured, pillaged and sunk by pirates.

SITE #81

SPANISH GALLEON OFF VENICE BEACH

An unidentified Spanish galleon lies in fairly shallow water about three-quarters of a mile due west of Venice Beach. The wreck is believed to be the source of the coins that wash up on the beach every now and then, mainly after storms.

SITE #82

GERMAN SUBMARINE AT OSPREY (1942)

A German U-boat sunk during World War II by bombs dropped by U.S. aircraft lies in about 65 feet of water west of the town of Osprey, north of Venice. At the time she went down, the sub carried $50,000 in gold.

SITE #83

SPANISH SHIP IN AN OCEAN SPRING (1700's)

A Spanish ship lies at the mouth of a freshwater spring in the Gulf of Mexico about 12 miles west of Sarasota. Divers report that the ship is in an excellent state of preservation due to the presence of fresh water.

This ship probably sank during a storm in the 1700's and is likely to have been carrying Spanish gold and silver from the New World.

SITE #84

CONFEDERATE SHIP AT BRADENTON BEACH (1863)

A Confederate blockade runner lies in the channel between the northern tip of Longboat Key and the southern end of Bradenton Beach.

During the Civil War, Union ships kept watch over Tampa Bay by blockading the shipping channels. This blockade runner made regular trips into the bay where she sold her supplies to the Confederates and then carefully and quickly made her way back into the Gulf. On one occasion, however, after delivering her merchandise she was spotted by a Union gunboat which sank her.

Since the blockade runner went down after selling her cargo, it is likely she was carrying a substantial amount of gold on board. The Confederates had no established credit and all payments had to be made in gold.

SITE #85

GERMAN SUBMARINE OFF BRADENTON BEACH (1944)

About six miles due west of Bradenton Beach in approximately 60 feet of water lies another German U-boat sunk during World War II.

SITE #86

BLOCKADE RUNNERS OFF ANNA MARIA ISLAND (1865)

Toward the end of the Civil War, at least five blockade runners were sunk by a Union gunboat just north of the island of Anna Maria west of Bradenton.

SITE #87

UNIDENTIFIED SPANISH GALLEON

About six miles due west of Anna Maria Island lies the wreck of a Spanish galleon. While little is known about the ship, it was probably part of the ill-fated Spanish fleet of 1715 which sank during a hurricane just west of the entrance to Tampa Bay.

It is likely that when the galleon went down, it carried to the bottom many of the riches of the New World which had been bound for Spain.

Treasure Markings
TR. BELOW
TR IN DIVIDED LOCATION
POINTS TO TREASURE
DOUBLE DISTANCE
EYE LOOKING AT TR.
WALKING TO TR.
POINTS TO TR.
TR ON LEFT
TR ON RIGHT
LOOKING AT TR.
TR BELOW
TR IN TRIANGLE
SAME
SNAKE POINTS TO TR.
TO OTHER SIGNS
NEAR WATER
TR IN CAVE
POINTS TO TR.
TR IN TRIANGLE
STAIRS
TR UND. HOUSE
TR IN BOX
GOLD BARS
1760 DATE OF BURIAL
ANCHOR TR. BELOW
TR IN LAKE
TR UNDER ROCK.
BOW & ARROW POINTS TO TR
TOWARD TR.
TR BELOW
7 GOLD
5 SILVER
3 JEWELS
TREASURE OFF
POINTS TO TR.
POINTS TO TR.
SNAKE IN TR. HEAD POINTS
CHEST ON TR. TRES BELOW.
BELOW ON LEFT

Southwestern Florida: Tampa Bay Area

SITE #88

BRITISH MERCHANT SHIP (1800)

A three-masted British schooner sank in 1800 during a hurricane in Tampa Bay. She is located about a mile east of the Sunshine Skyway Bridge, which links St. Petersburg with the Sarasota-Bradenton area.

SITE #89

SPANISH GALLEON AT THE SUNSHINE SKYWAY (1715)

A Spanish galleon lies under the second large piling under the main span of the Sunshine Skyway bridge, north of the shipping channel. She is believed to be one of the 1715 fleet that entered Tampa Bay to escape a storm in the Gulf of Mexico but ultimately sank all the same. Like her sister ships who shared her fate, she was carrying a full load of gold bars and coins bound for the Spanish royal court.

SITE #90

BRITISH PAY SHIP (1814)

During the War of 1812, a British payroll ship sailing from Jamaica to New Orleans with money to pay the troops and civilians in that city never arrived at her destination. Instead, she battled with an American warship just south of the entrance to Tampa Bay. The British ship was badly damaged and limped into the bay, anchoring about three-quarters of a mile southeast of the municipal pier. Her crew tried desperately to save her from sinking, but her end was inevitable. She went down with $50,000 in British gold and silver coins.

SITE #91

RIVIERA BAY WRECK (1824)

The pirate Henry Ross hid a boatload of stolen silver bars out in the middle of Tampa Bay by anchoring her fore and aft and then boring holes in her hull. He never reclaimed his sunken treasure. Today, she rests in Riviera Bay just south of the Gandy Bridge.

SITE #92

GANDY BRIDGE WRECK

Another shipwreck lies in the mud about 1000 feet from the western end of Gandy Bridge and 300 feet to the north. A jumble of iron cannons rests near her.

SITE #93

AIRPORT WRECK

In Old Tampa Bay, east of the north runway at St. Petersburg-Clearwater International Airport, lies a shipwreck with six brass cannons on deck and silver bars and coins in her hold. Some artifacts have been recovered but much awaits the treasure seeker.

SITE #94

SILVER BAR WRECK

Just west of Site No. 93 in old Tampa Bay is the wreck of an unnamed ship that is believed to have been carrying $600,000 in silver bars when she went down.

SITE #95

DE SOTO'S SHIP (1529)

Located at the northern end of Old Tampa Bay in Safety Harbor is the wreckage of a 450-year-old ship thought to have belonged to the Spanish explorer Hernando de Soto. It is known the explorer lost at least one ship during his stay in Tampa Bay in 1529.

When she went down during a hurricane, the ship was carrying a sufficient amount of gold and silver coins to pay the wages of 400 men. She is no doubt worth a salvage effort.

SITE #96

SAILING SKIFF IN LITTLE MANATEE RIVER (1763)

In 1763, map maker Bernard Romans deliberately sank his small sailing skiff at the mouth of the Little Manatee River, intending to return for her later after completing an overland trek to St. Augustine. Romans is the man who mapped Florida for the British during their 20-year occupation of the state from 1763 to 1783.

Documents reveal that the map maker never returned to raise and recover his boat. What remains of it would make an historical find of note.

SITE #97

TWO-MAN GERMAN SUBMARINE (1945)

A two-man German submarine lies in about 18 feet of water approximately one mile east of Egmont Key. In 1945, a Coast Guard commander had been given orders to sink the captured "baby" U-boat. The choice of a site was left up to him. Since the commander's crew needed target practice, he had the sub anchored fore and aft at low tide off Egmont Key where they sank it with 12 six-inch shells.

SITE #98

PIRATE SHIP IN THE MANATEE RIVER (1824)

In 1824, a United States Navy vessel spotted a pirate named Miguel Guerrie pillaging a merchant ship in the Gulf of Mexico. Seeing the Navy ship, the pirate and his crew hastily set sail toward Tampa Bay, with their pursuer close behind them. The pirates fled into the Manatee River where they finally ran aground. The crew jumped overboard and hiked to safety by foot.

When the naval ship arrived, the sailors set the pirate ship on fire and abandoned her. Silver bars have been found at the site and more are believed to be in the area.

SITE #99

BRASS CANNONS AT THE MOUTH OF THE MANATEE RIVER

It is believed 18 brass cannons filled with pirate treasure are to be found under the sand at the mouth of the Manatee River. Jean Lafitte may have fitted the cannons with his loot, sealed them with wooden plugs and dumped them overboard, no doubt intending to collect his holdings later.

SITE #100

LAFITTE'S SHIP IN OLD TAMPA BAY (1824)

The remains of one of pirate Jean Lafitte's ships lies at the bottom of Old Tampa Bay about three-quarters of a mile southwest of Rocky Point, west of the Tampa International Airport. Lafitte had been chased by a U.S. warship into the bay and when the pirate could run no further, he turned and fought until the larger vessel sank his ship. The crafty pirate and his crew managed to swim ashore and escaped capture.

SITE #101

SIGHTING OF AN OLD SHIP

In 1893, a merchant was making his weekly trip to Tampa in a small sailing skiff to purchase supplies, when through unusually clear water he saw a well preserved hull of an ancient ship. The merchant thought he knew the area so well that he would have no trouble finding the site again but to his dismay, he never again found the ship. No doubt what he had seen was a freak of nature — shifting sands had temporarily uncovered the wreck and then hidden it once more, where it remains today somewhere in old Tampa Bay.

SITE #102

BLOCKADE RUNNER AT HILLSBOROUGH RIVER (1862)

In 1862, a Confederate schooner loaded with supplies sailed toward Fort Brooke which was then held by the South. A Union warship followed and sank the blockade runner at the mouth of the Hillsborough River. Her loss was a severe blow to the Confederates occupying the fort and later led to their abandoning it.

SITE #103

PIRATE SHIPS AT HILLSBOROUGH RIVER (1821)

In 1821, a United States warship chased a pirate ship all the way from the Gulf of Mexico to the Hillsborough River. About two miles up river from Hillsborough Bay, the pirate ship ran aground. To escape capture and the inevitable hanging, the pirates jumped overboard and escaped into the heavy foliage along the banks of the waterway.

The Americans who had been trailing the ship boarded and set her on fire. She burned to the waterline, taking to the bottom any valuables in her hold.

SITE #104

LOST PROPELLER IN SHIPPING CHANNEL (1942)

In 1942, a merchant ship on her way up the bay to deliver cargo at Port Tampa lost a large eight-foot bronze propeller weighing thousands of pounds. Considering the high price of scrap metal today, it could bring in a nice bit of money.

SITE #105

WRECK OF THE "MARIA THERESA II" (1824)

The wreck at the mouth of Tampa Bay is thought to be the Maria Theresa II, which belonged to a pirate named Bartholomew Roberts who was associated with the infamous Jean Lafitte. Roberts was believed to be returning from Charlotte Harbor where he had dug up a considerable amount of loot, bound for New Orleans. Unfortunately for him, a British warship followed in pursuit and during the ensuing battle, the Maria Theresa sank. Her treasures went down with her.

Notes

Central Gulf Coast: North of Tarpon Springs

SITE #106

BAILEY'S BLUFF WRECK

An unidentified wreck lies just to the west of Bailey's Bluff, north of the Anclote River. This ship is believed to be the source of the coins that wash up on the shore after storms.

SITE #107

BARGE AT GREEN KEY

An old steel barge rests at the bottom of the south side of Green Key, just west of New Port Richey.

SITE #108

PADDLE-WHEELER AT GREEN KEY (1873)

In 1873, a paddle-wheel steamer on its way from New Orleans to Tampa with passengers and freight ran aground on some rocks along the northwest side of Green Key. For many years, brass ship's spikes, steam gauges and other artifacts have been found by divers. The ship's safe may still be under the sand.

SITE #109

UNKNOWN WRECK NORTHWEST OF GREEN KEY

The wreck of an old Spanish galleon is located about three miles northwest of Green Key. It is encrusted with coral rock but underneath much of the ship is still intact.

SITE #110

WRECK AT ARIPEKA

Another unidentified shipwreck lies in Indian Bay just north of Aripeka. It is believed to have a cargo of gold coins.

SITE #111

WRECK AT THE MOUTH OF MUD RIVER

Mud River originates in Weeki Wachee Springs and empties into the Gulf at Bayport. The wreck, which lies at the river's mouth, is thought to have been a blockade runner carrying war materials which was sunk by a Union gunboat.

SITE #112

BLOCKADE RUNNER AT HOMOSASSA (1863)

This Confederate blockade runner was sunk by the Union warship U.S.S. Hatteras at the mouth of the Homosassa River in the Spring of 1863. The Confederate ship is believed to be the Mary Jane, which was transporting war material to the plantation of Senator David Yulee.

SITE #113

"EDWARD MACEY" WRECK AT GHOST ISLAND (1843)

In the fall of 1843, the schooner Edward Macey was on her way from Mobile, Alabama, to New York with a load of lumber when she struck a rock during a storm and tore open her hull. The captain and crew escaped to a nearby island where they all proceeded to get drunk. During an argument, the captain grabbed a cut glass and cut off the mate's head. The next morning, the remaining survivors buried the body along with the ship's strongbox. They then rowed to the mainland in the ship's lifeboat and went their separate ways.

Local residents say that a headless ghost walks the island on moonlit nights, looking for its head. They say if you watch where the ghost disappears into the ground, you will find the location of the strongbox. No map site.

SITE #114

WRECK AT THE WITHLACOOCHEE RIVER

At the mouth of the Withlacoochee River near Yankeetown is an old galleon loaded with silver bars. For years local fisherman made net weights out of them thinking they were lead.

SITE #115

SPANISH GALLEON AT WACCASSA BAY

At the mouth of the Waccassa River is the wreckage of an Old Spanish galleon. No more is known about her.

SITE #116

WRECK AT ROCKY RUN CREEK

Another small wreck, possibly a Confederate blockade runner, lies at the mouth of Rocky Creek which empties into Waccassa Bay.

Notes

Northwestern Florida: Mouth of the Suwannee River

SITE #117

CONFEDERATE GUN BOAT (1864)

A Confederate ship left Galveston, Texas, in October 1864 with $25 million in gold. Her final destination was supposed to have been Havana, Cuba, where the gold would have been transferred to a British ship and taken to London. If this Confederate fortune had gotten through safely, some speculate that the Civil War might have lasted another 10 years.

Instead, Union agents got wind of the plot and informed Northern naval authorities, who had warships waiting to tail the Confederate vessel. Realizing that their capture was near, the Confederate captain issued orders to head for the Suwannee River. Meanwhile, the crew started jettisoning the gold overboard as they tried to sail toward safety. But the ship ran aground at a turn in the river and the captain gave orders to abandon ship.

People have looked for the lost gold from the Confederate ship for years. A few pieces have been found but the bulk of the treasure waits for some lucky individual to find it, scattered in the Suwannee River.

Notes

Florida Panhandle

SITE #118

BLOCKADE RUNNER IN DEADMAN BAY (1864)

Located just off Lazy Island in picturesquely named Deadman Bay are the remains of a Confederate blockade runner. The three-masted schooner, dated from 1864, judging from artifacts that have been found, was about 90 to 120 feet long. She carried a load of small brass cannons for field use, plus a good supply of cannon balls, gun powder and medical supplies. Her cargo, however, never reached its destination. Instead, she was sunk by the United States warship Vincennes who also captured and imprisoned her crew in Key West, the Union ship's home port.

SITE #119

WRECK OF THE "MARY ANDERS" (1796)

The Mary Anders was a British merchant ship on her way from New Orleans to Liverpool, England, with a load of Mexican silver. She sailed into a hurricane and her captain, sensing disaster, ordered her strongbox taken ashore and buried. The ship sank with the silver still on board.

She lies just offshore from Dog Island, on the Gulf side. The island is south of the town of Carrabelle along the Panhandle.

SITE #120

SHIP OF SILVER OFF DOG ISLAND

This ship was captured by pirate Billy Bowlegs and hauled into St. George's Sound to the north of Dog Island. Billy's men removed her rigging and masts, anchored her fore and aft, tore holes in her hull and let her gradually sink to the bottom. The pirates assumed they would return for the ship's cargo of silver bars; they never did.

SITE #121

BILLY BOWLEG'S SHIP (1821)

It wasn't Billy's day back in 1821. A warship caught his ship out at sea in the act of piracy and chased the band of thieves toward the Panhandle. The warship sank the pirate ship off Dog Island on the Gulf side, near East Pass. The pirates swarmed over the sides, swam to shore and disappeared into the heavy foliage along the coast.

SITE #122

SILVER BAR WRECK

This wreck is similar to one at Site No. 120. Pirates deliberately sank a captured ship loaded with silver bars, hoping to return later and claim their prize. The wreck is located in St. George Sound off Dog Island.

SITE #123

WRECK OF THE "WILLIE JONES" (1863)

The Willie Jones was trying to run the Union blockade in July 1863 with a load of war material when she was caught in the East Pass between Dog Island and St. George Island. Union forces sank her there, though her crew managed to swim ashore to Dog Island.

SITE #124

H.M.S. SCHOONER "FOX" (1799)

The British ship Fox was carrying Englishman William Augustus Bowles and his staff to west Florida in August, 1799, when she hit a reef and sank just offshore from the eastern end of St. George Island. Bowles, who had been sent to Florida to stir up trouble between the Indians there and the white settlers to the north, swam to shore along with his officers and crew members. They lived the life of Robinson Crusoe for many months until a British warship, which had been sent to look for them, rescued the group.

The Fox went down with $200,000 in gold which was to have been used by Bowles for his clandestine operation.

SITE #125

RUM RUNNER OFF ST. GEORGE ISLAND (1800)

About 10 miles west of the site of the H.M.S. Fox is the wreckage of another schooner. This ship had been carrying 200 barrels of West Indian rum when it went down during a hurricane in 1800. That liquor would certainly be well aged by now.

SITE #126

BARGE OFF ST. GEORGE ISLAND (1931)

About a mile offshore from the middle of St. George Island is a steel barge loaded with lead bars. She had been traveling from New Orleans to Tampa in 1931 when a hurricane sank her. The lead is worth salvaging.

SITE #127

BLOCKADE RUNNER OFF APALACHICOLA (1862)

The wreckage of a Confederate blockade runner lies in Apalachicola Bay, off the mainland. Since Confederate paper money was considered worthless overseas, blockade runners were forced to buy and sell using U.S. or British gold coins. As a result, they frequently carried large sums of gold as they made their daring forays through enemy lines. It is likely this ship went down with a substantial fortune. No map site.

SITE #128

WRECK AT WEST PASS (1819)

Documents show that a ship belonging to pirate Billy Bowlegs was sunk by a British frigate in 1819 as the pirate vessel attempted to sail out into the Gulf of Mexico from West Pass. The pass is located between St. George Island and St. Vincent Island. She went down with Billy's stolen silver and coins.

SITE #129

WRECK OF THE "EMPIRE MICA" (1943)

The modern steel ship Empire Mica was sunk during World War II by a German submarine. The American ship lies on the Gulf side of Santa Rosa Island off the coast of Pensacola.

SITE #130

TUGBOAT "SIMPSON" (1933)

The tugboat Simpson sank along the Gulf side of Santa Rosa Island. The reason for her sinking is not known.

SITE #131

TUGBOAT "LEROY" (1933)

The LeRoy was a deep water tug that sank in about 110 feet of water south of Panama City during a hurricane in 1933. The crew was saved but the boat was a complete loss.

SITE #132

AMERICAN FREIGHTER "THE TARPON" (1932)

The Tarpon sank in about 100 feet of water during a 1932 hurricane. No map site.

SITE #133

SPANISH GALLEON WRECKS (1767)

The wreckage of five Spanish galleons lies at the center of Pensacola Bay, each of which was carrying at least a million dollars in New World gold, silver and gems when they went down during a hurricane in 1767.

EXCERPT FROM N.O.A.A. CHART NO. 11462

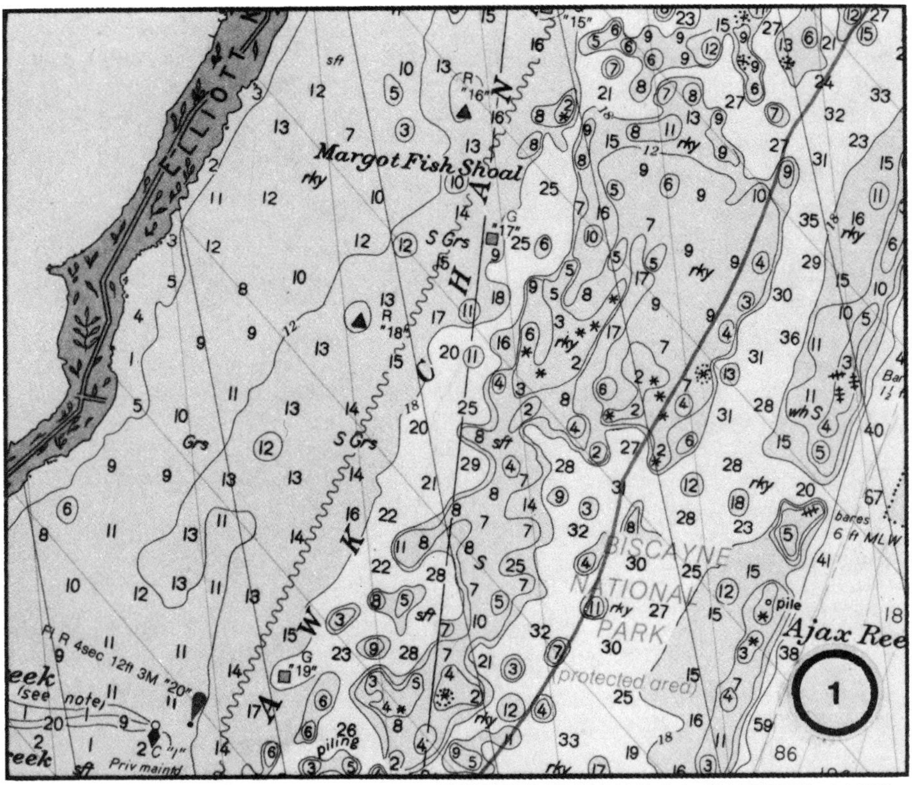

EXCERPT FROM N.O.A.A. CHART NO. 11462

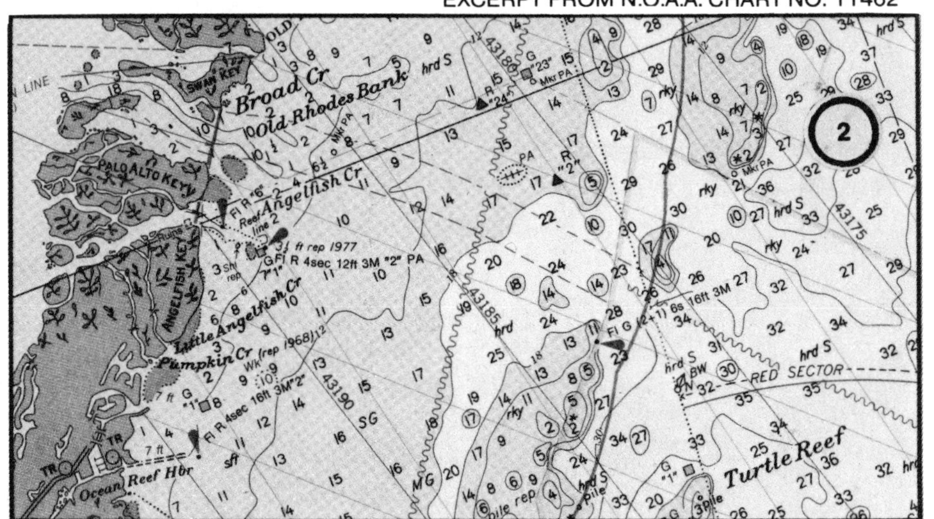

EXCERPT FROM N.O.A.A. CHART NO. 11462

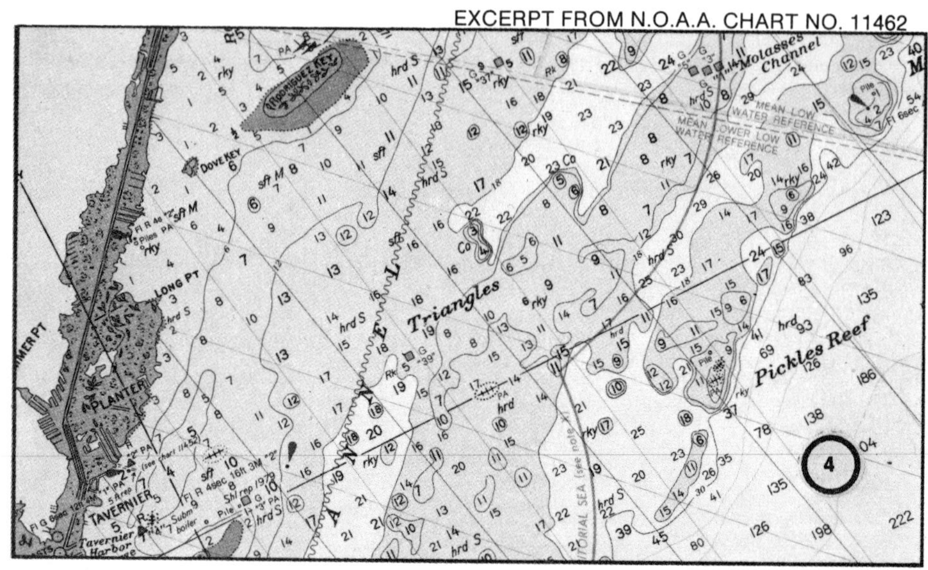

EXCERPT FROM N.O.A.A. CHART NO. 11452

EXCERPT FROM N.O.A.A. CHART NO. 11452

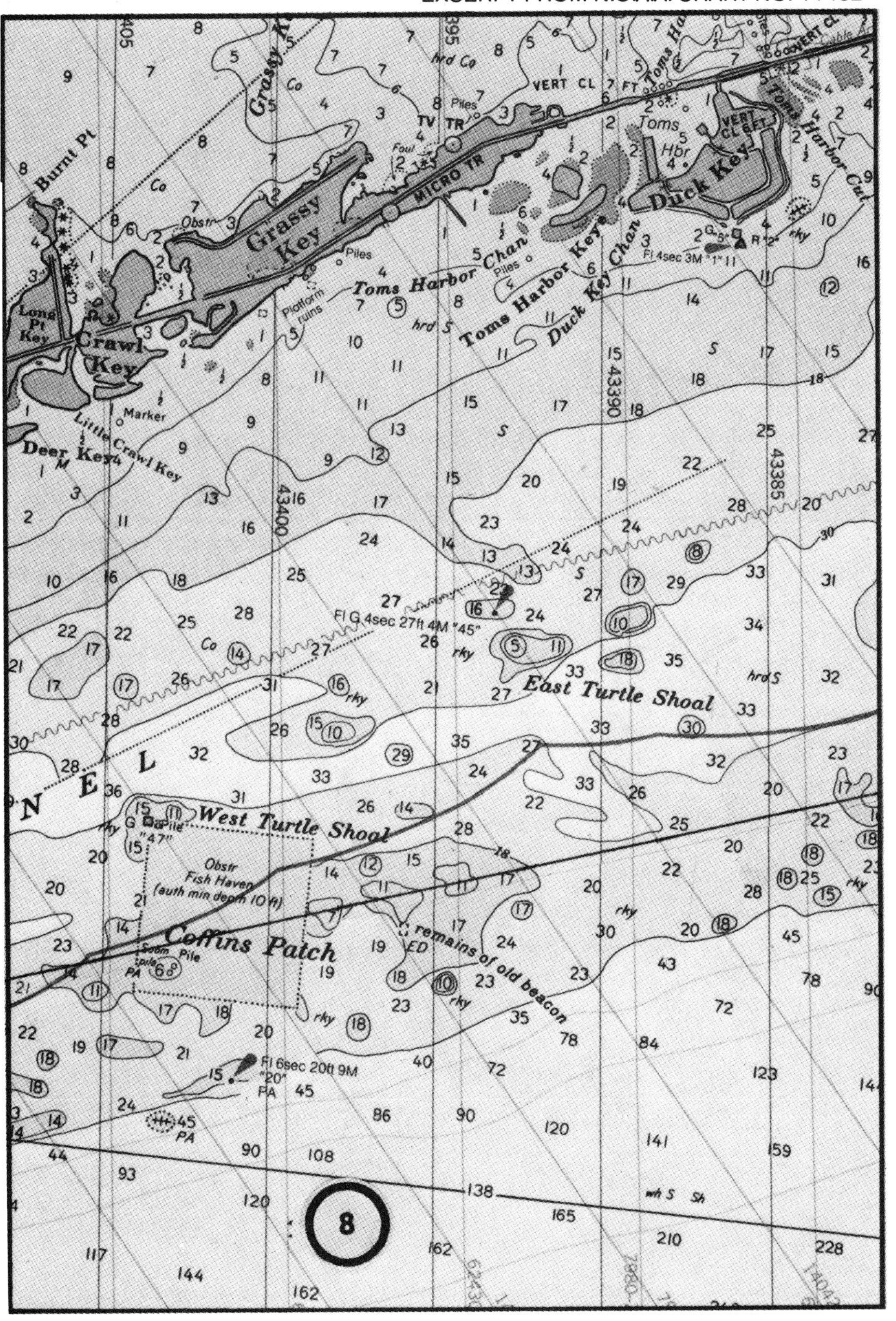

EXCERPT FROM N.O.A.A. CHART NO. 11452

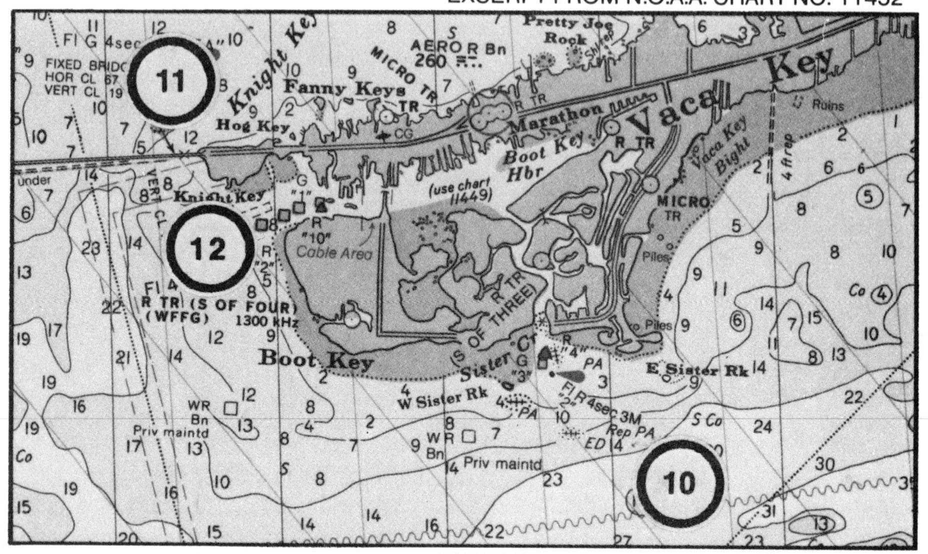

EXCERPT FROM N.O.A.A. CHART NO. 11442

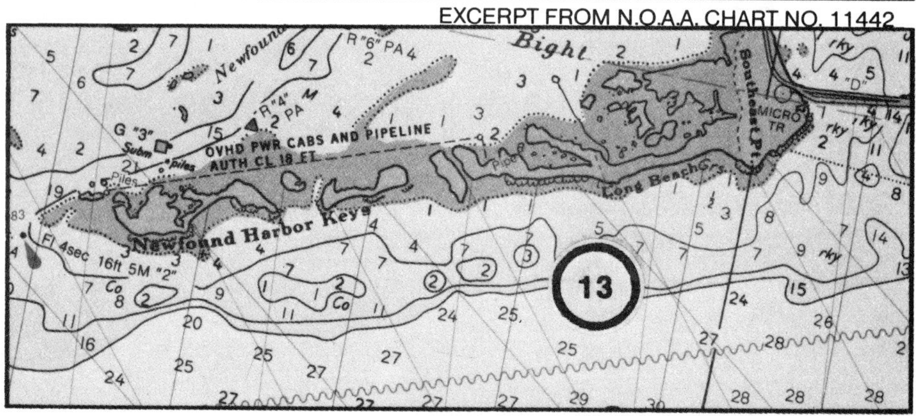

EXCERPT FROM N.O.A.A. CHART NO. 11442

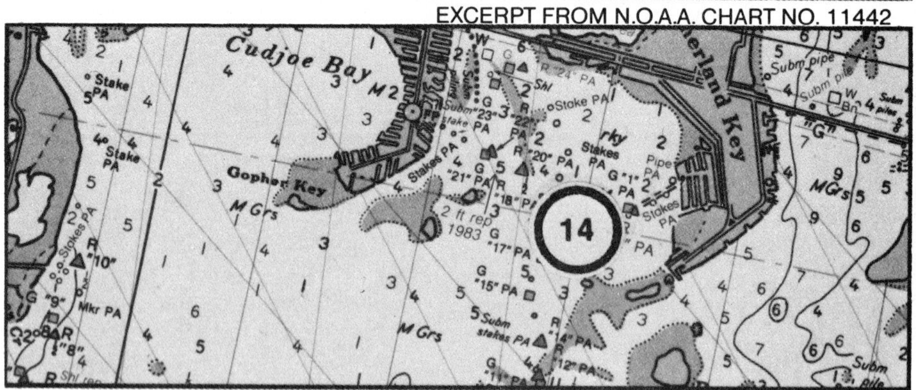

EXCERPT FROM N.O.A.A. CHART NO. 11442

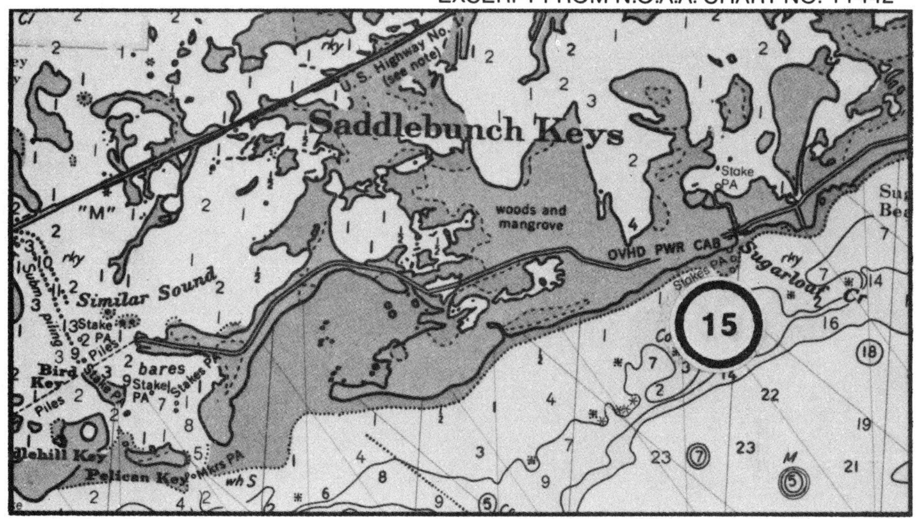

EXCERPT FROM N.O.A.A. CHART NO. 11452

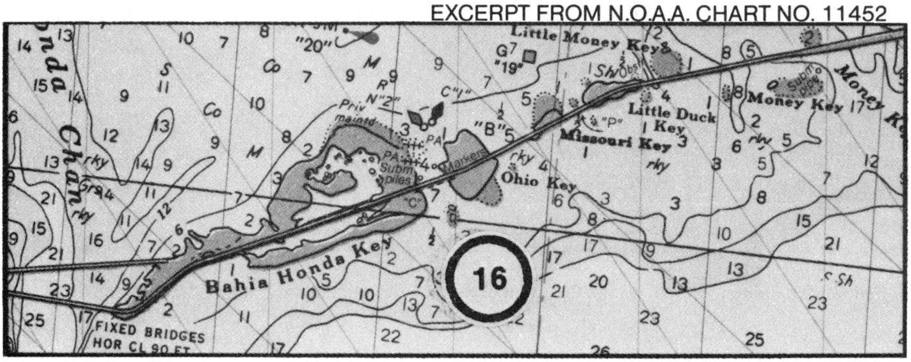

EXCERPT FROM N.O.A.A. CHART NO. 11445

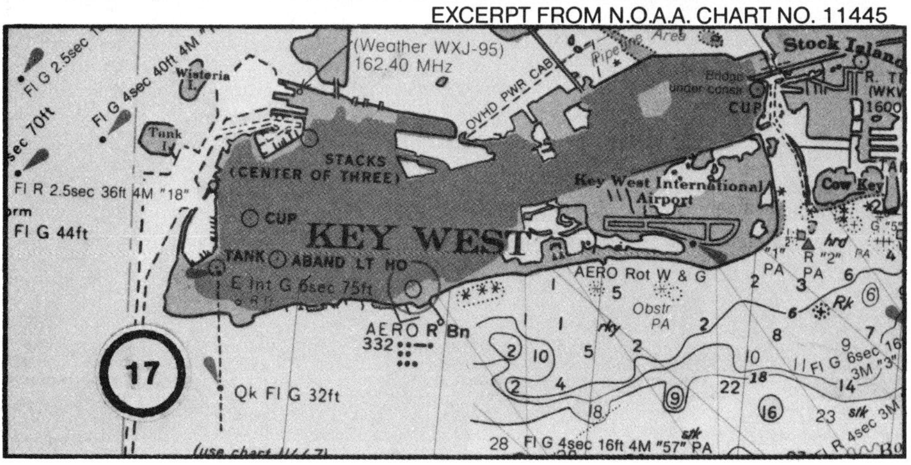

EXCERPT FROM N.O.A.A. CHART NO. 11434

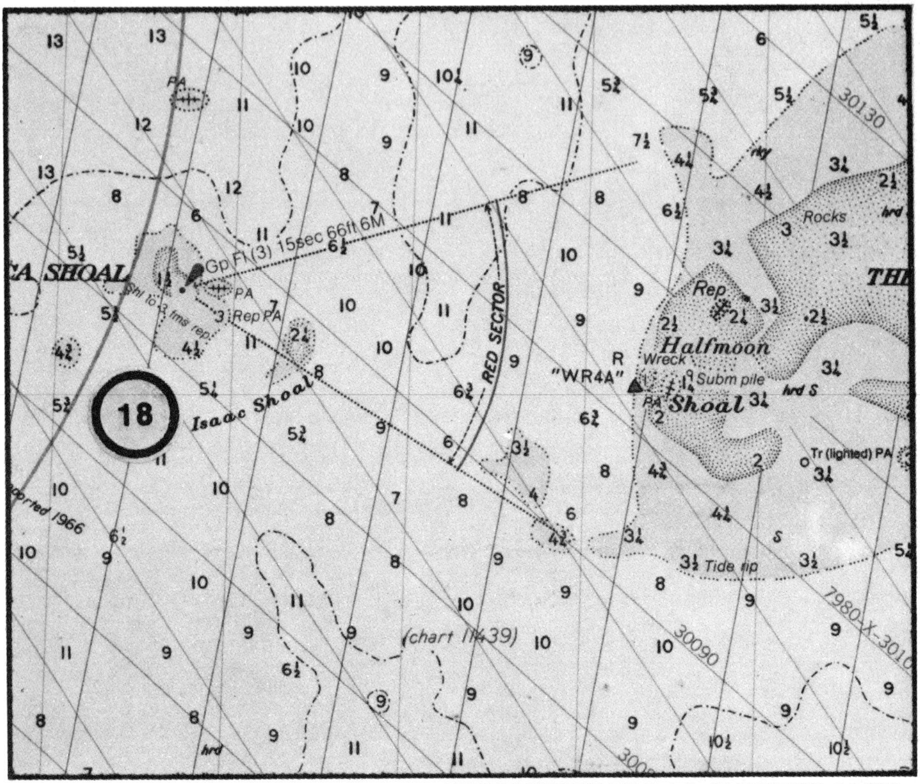

EXCERPT FROM N.O.A.A. CHART NO. 11438

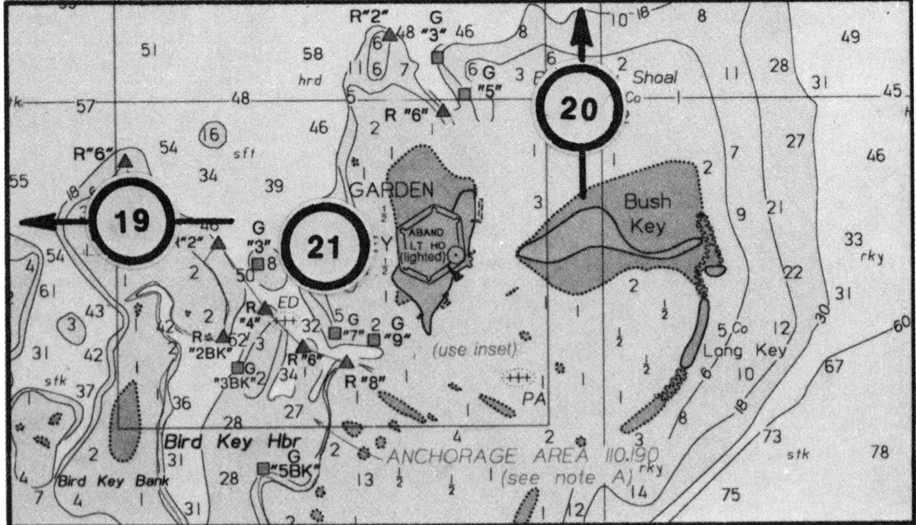

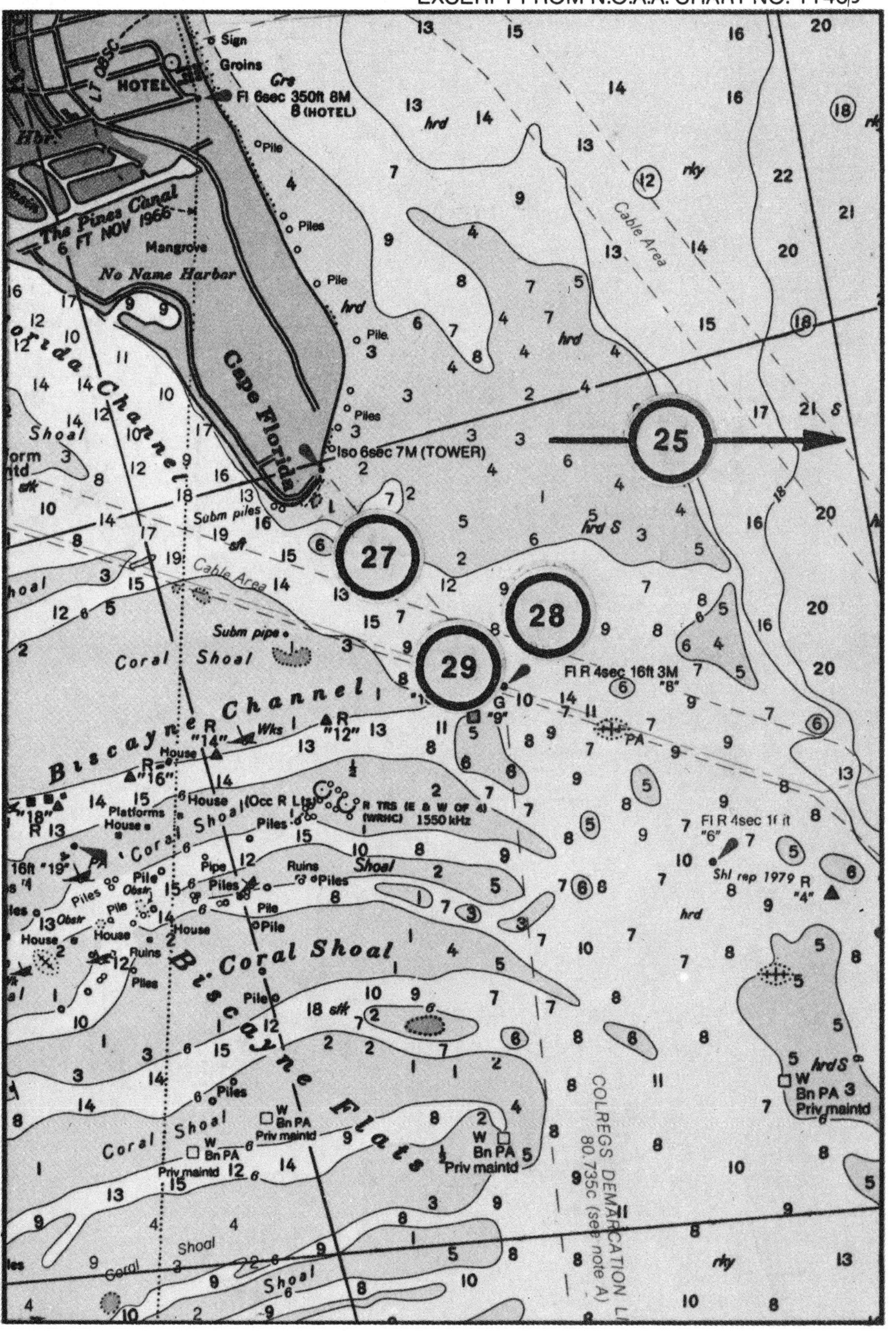

EXCERPT FROM N.O.A.A. CHART NO. 11465

EXCERPT FROM N.O.A.A. CHART NO. 11486

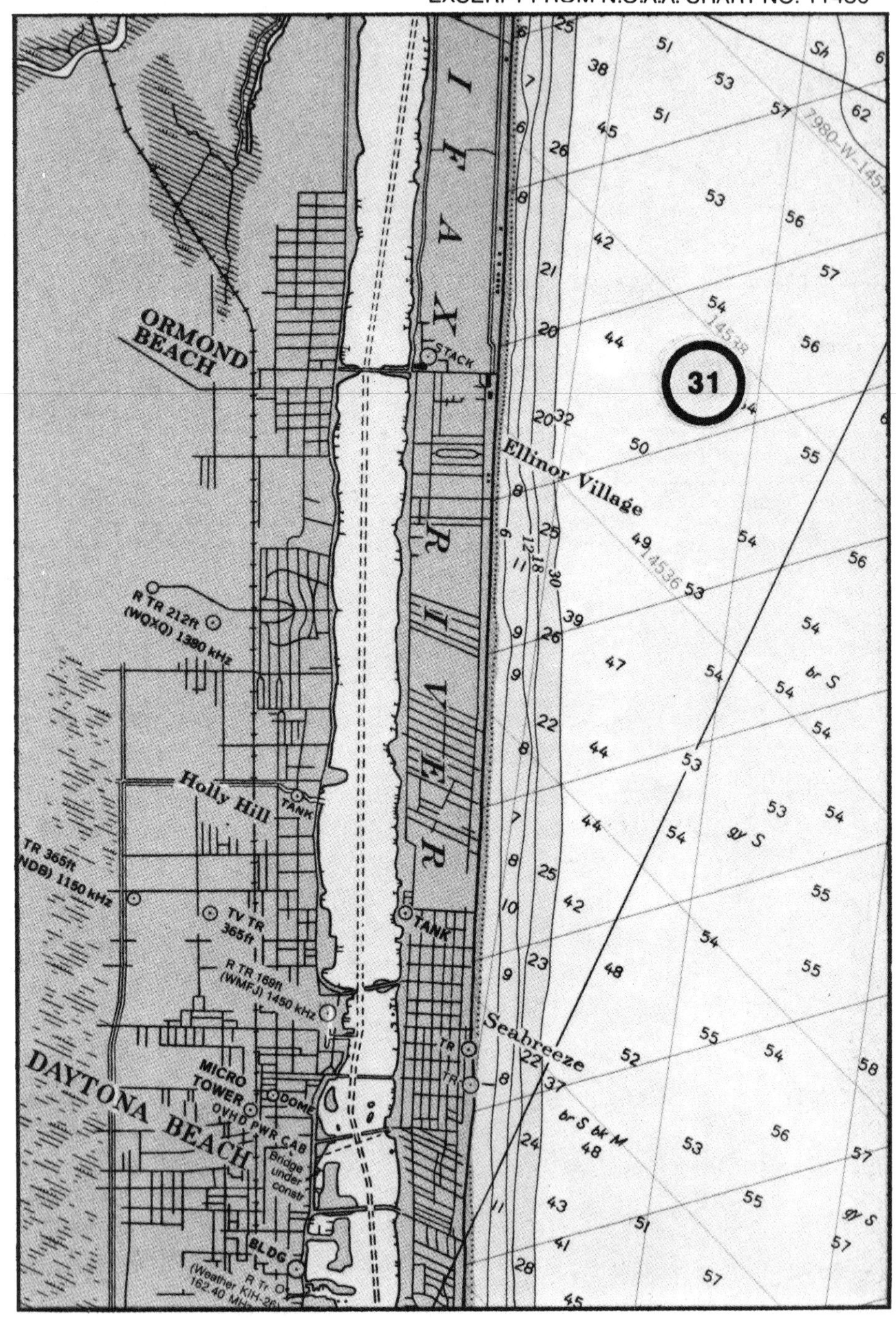

EXCERPT FROM N.O.A.A. CHART NO. 11484

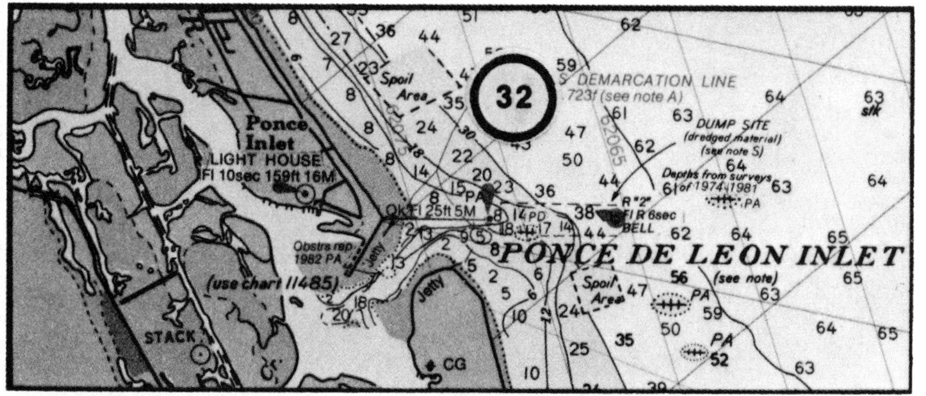

EXCERPT FROM N.O.A.A. CHART NO. 11484

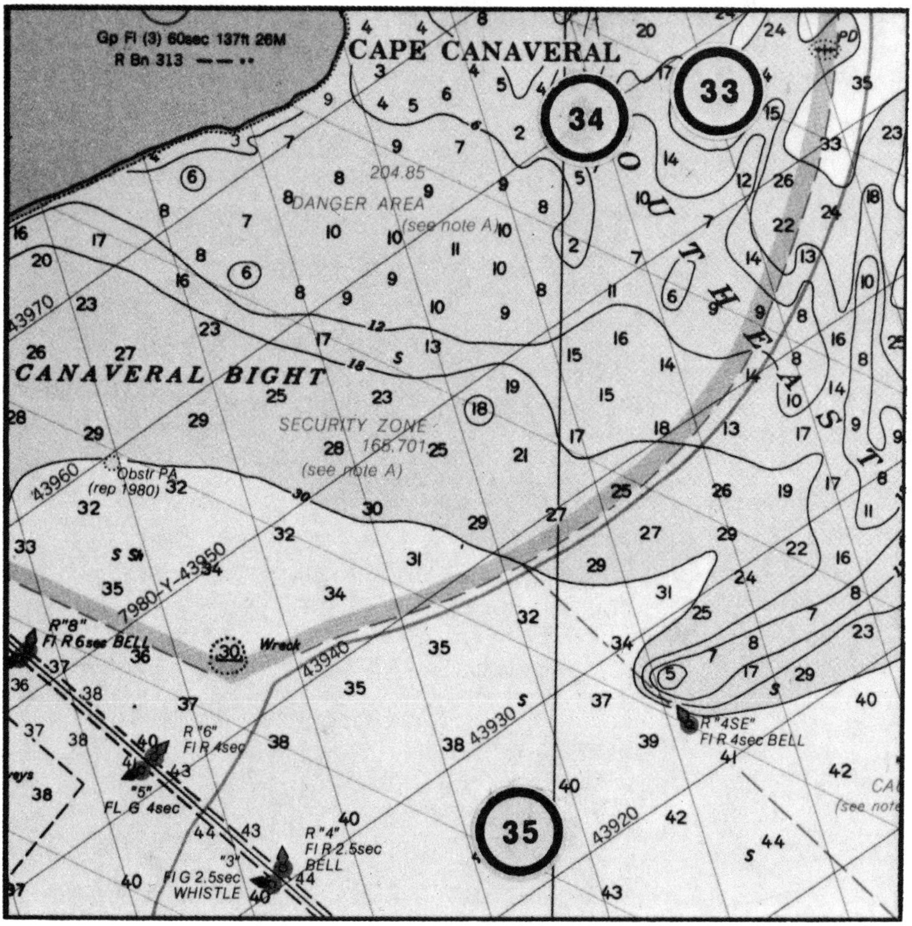

EXCERPT FROM N.O.A.A. CHART NO. 11474

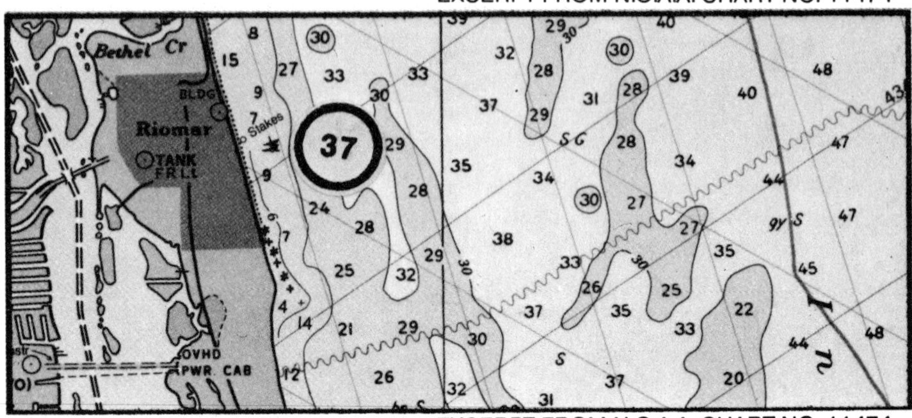

EXCERPT FROM N.O.A.A. CHART NO. 11474

EXCERPT FROM N.O.A.A. CHART NO. 11474

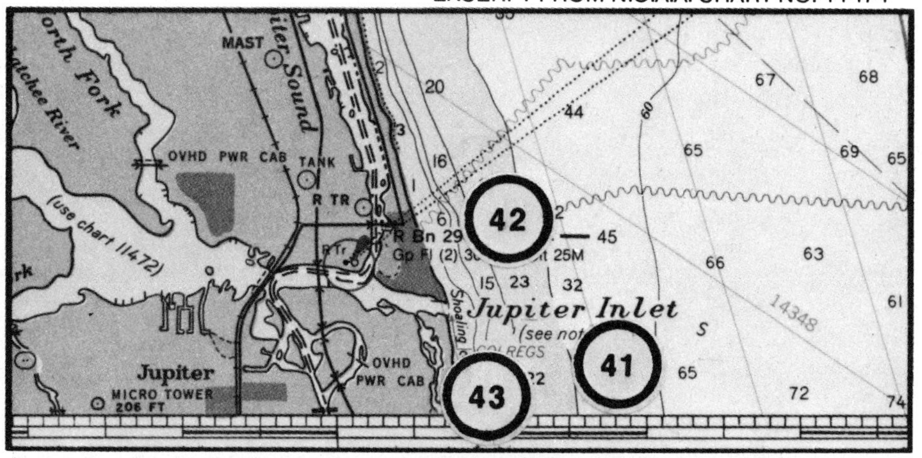

EXCERPT FROM N.O.A.A. CHART NO. 11486

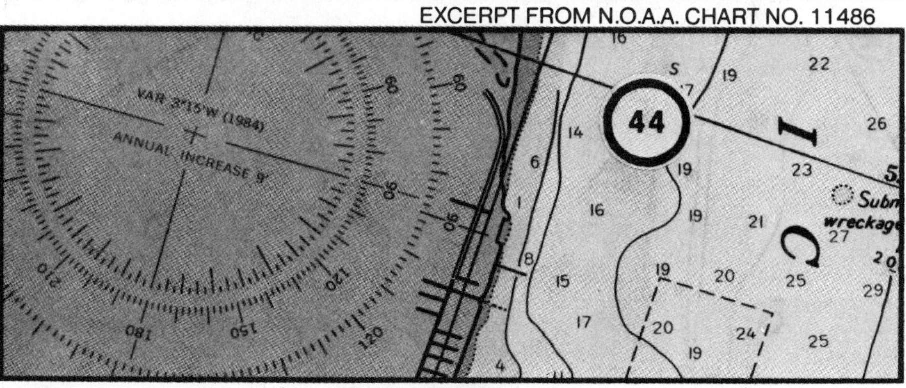

EXCERPT FROM N.O.A.A. CHART NO. 11485

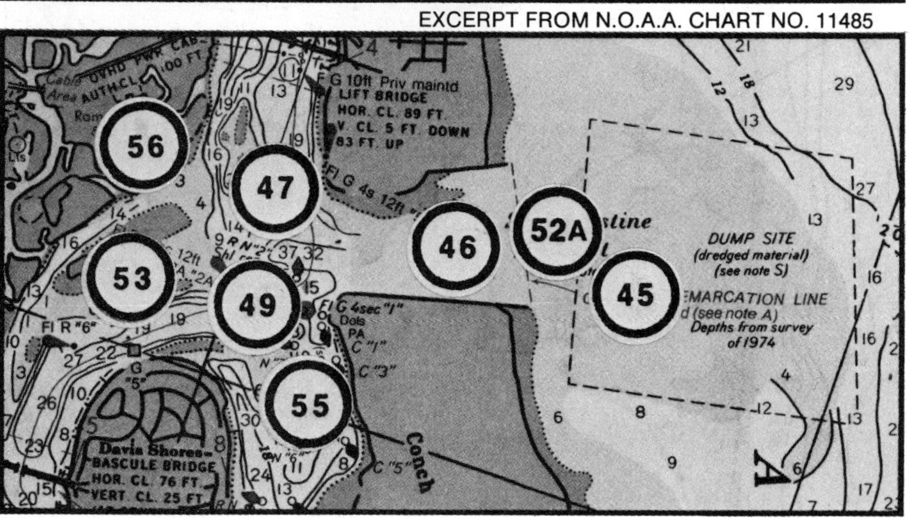

EXCERPT FROM N.O.A.A. CHART NO. 11486

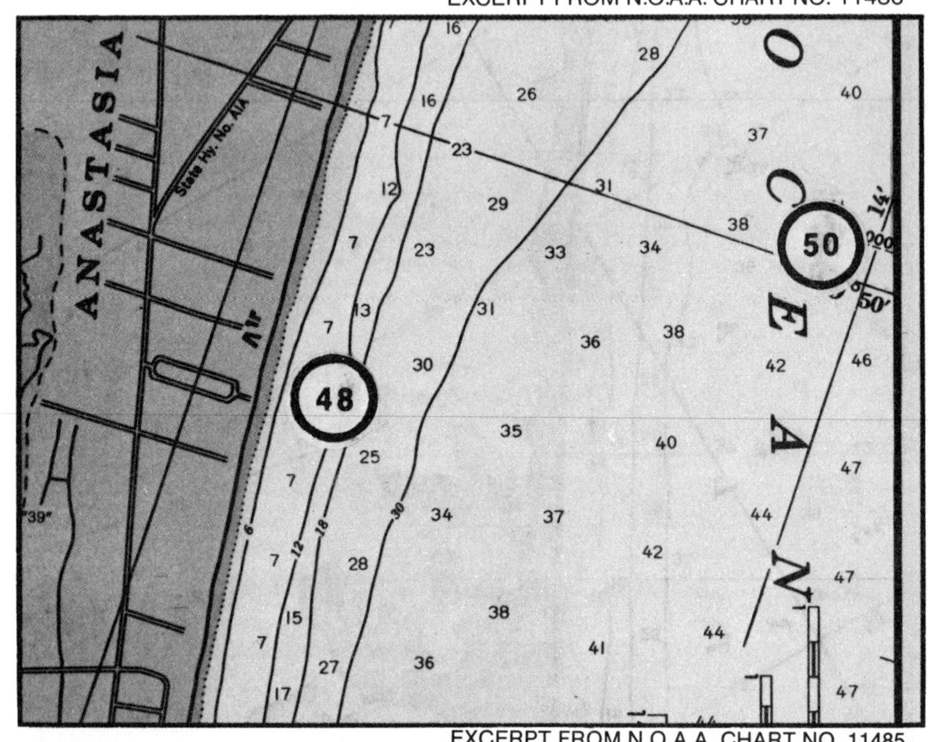

EXCERPT FROM N.O.A.A. CHART NO. 11485

NOTE E
The buoys marking
Salt Run are privately
maintained.

Salt Run

F Fl 30sec
161ft 19M

Cable Area

N SEBASTIAN RIVER
trolling depth of the improved
m the junction with the Intra-
aterway to the Kings Street
7½ feet for a width of 100 feet.
Sept.-Nov. 1968

CHART 11488

51

52

EXCERPT FROM N.O.A.A. CHART NO. 11488

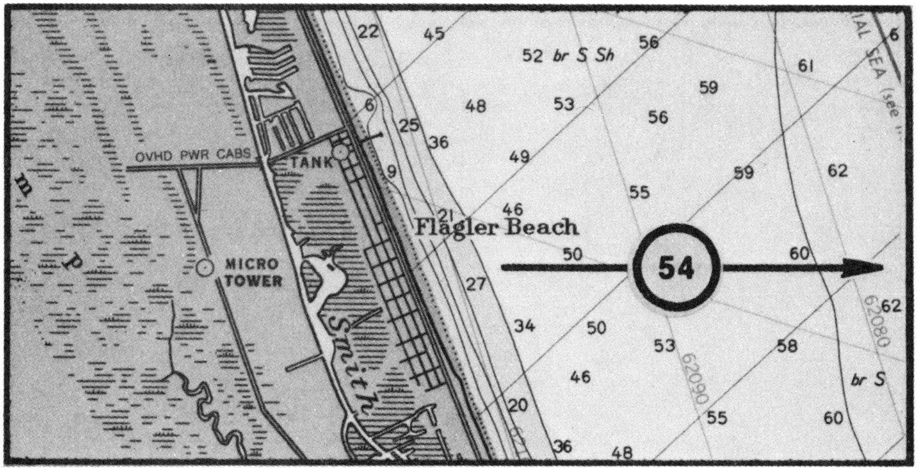

EXCERPT FROM N.O.A.A. CHART NO. 11485

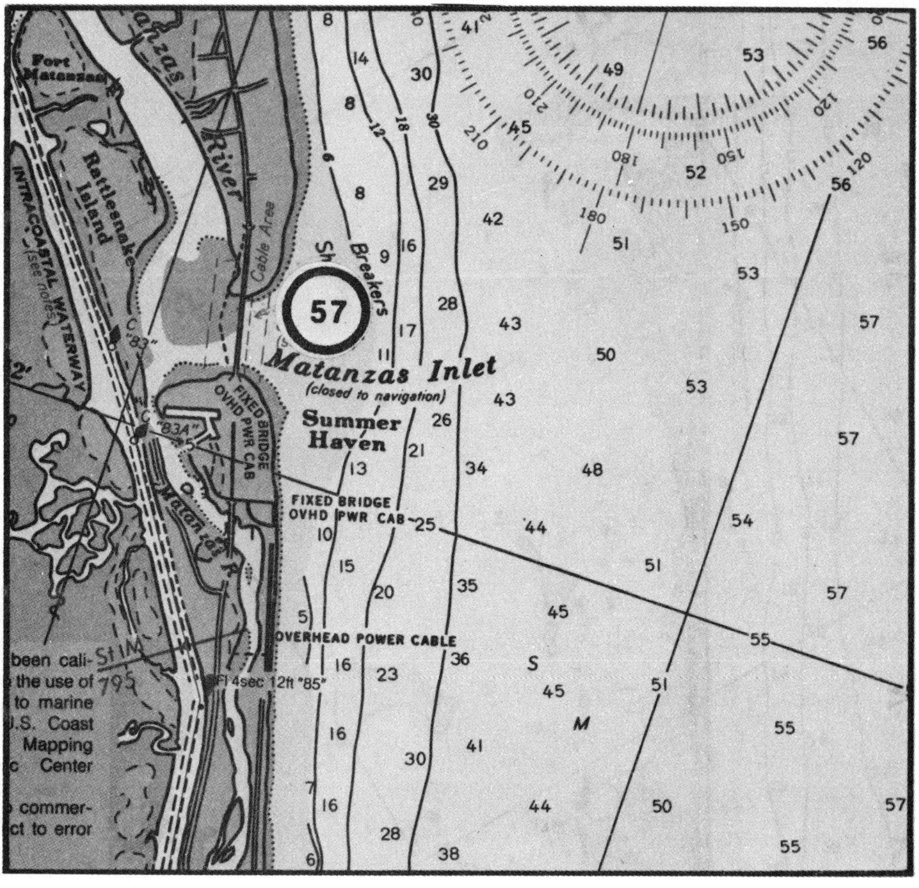

EXCERPT FROM N.O.A.A. CHART NO. 11502

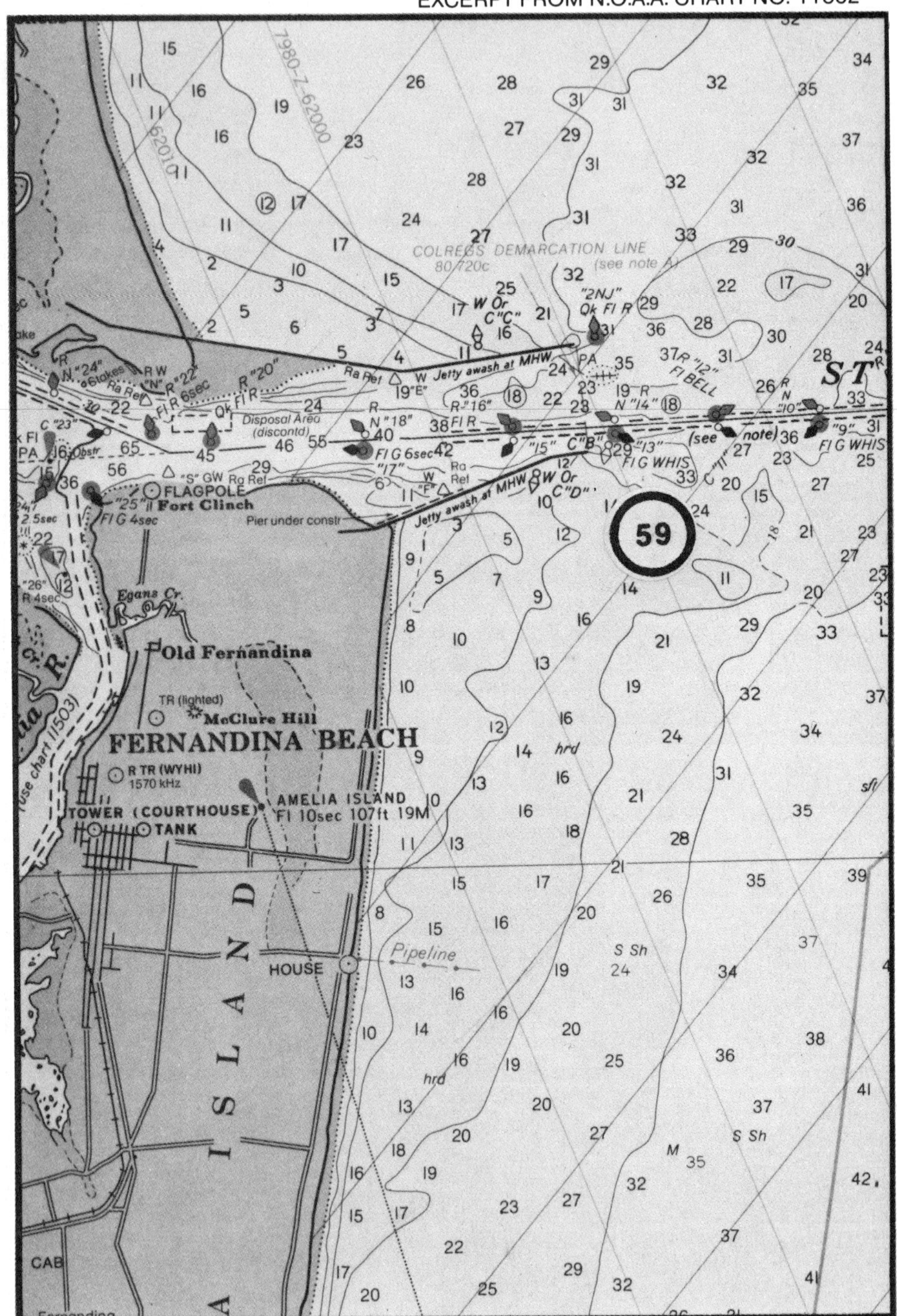

EXCERPT FROM N.O.A.A. CHART NO. 11488

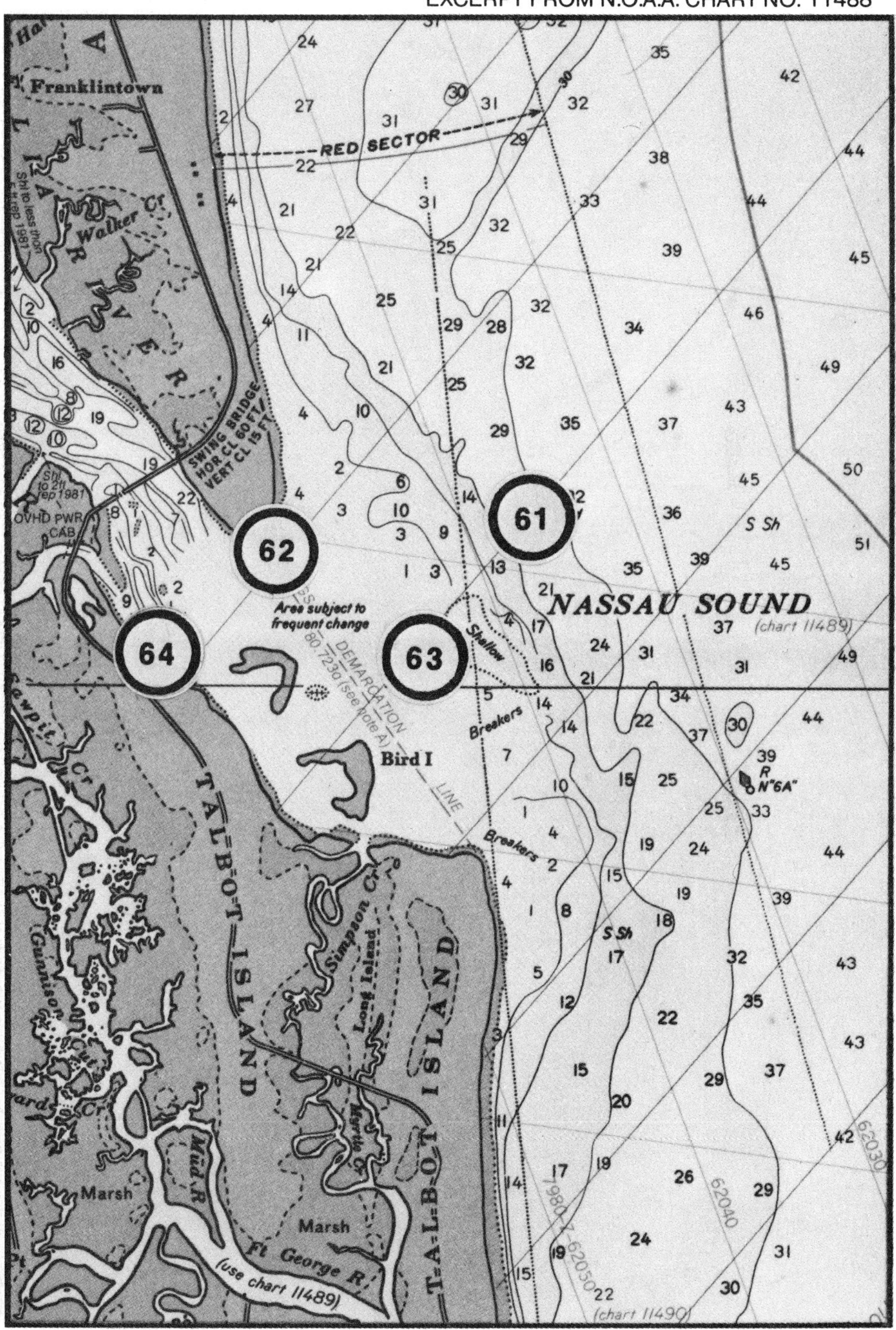

EXCERPT FROM N.O.A.A. CHART NO. 11433

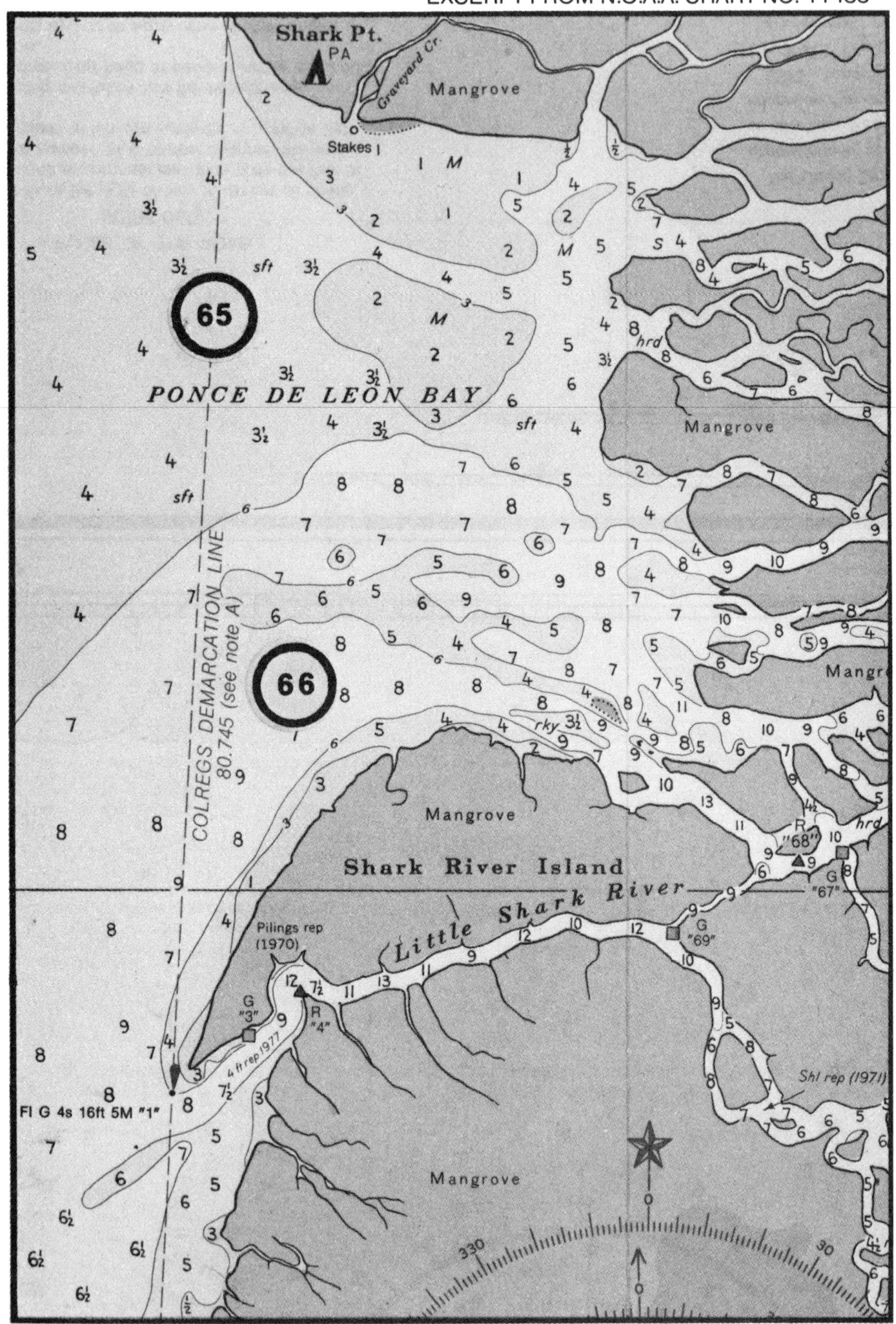

EXCERPT FROM N.O.A.A. CHART NO. 11432

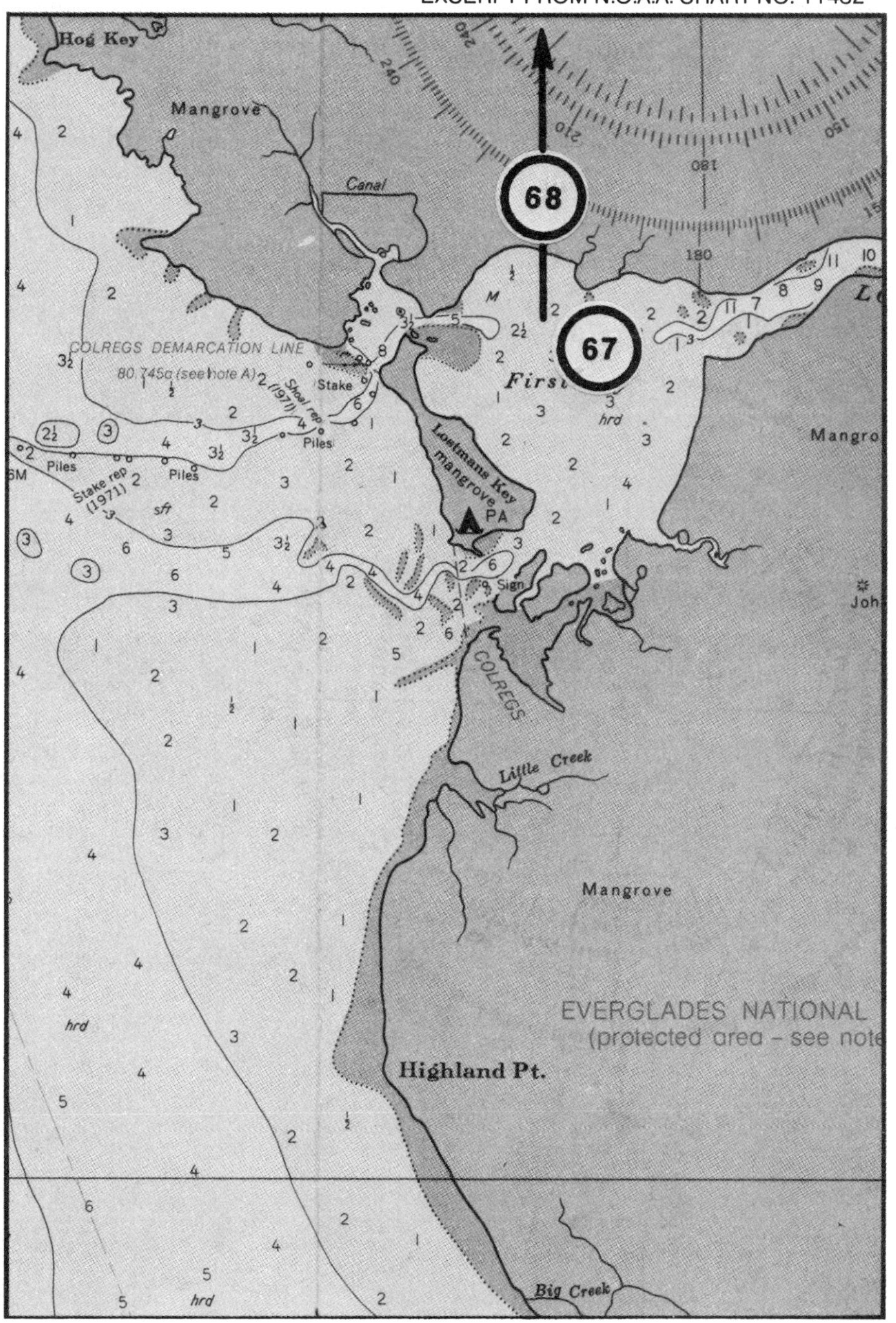

EXCERPT FROM N.O.A.A. CHART NO. 11429

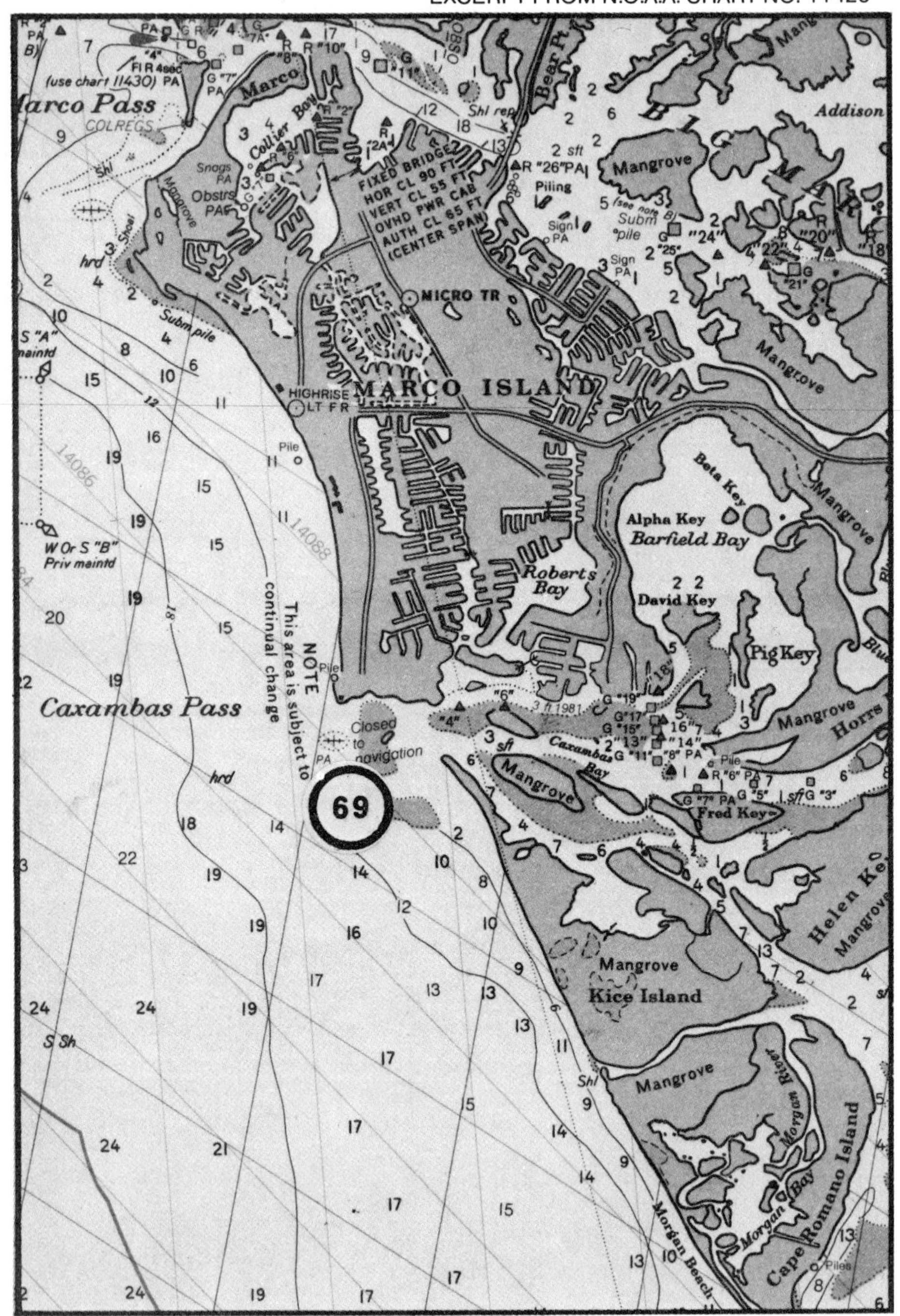

EXCERPT FROM N.O.A.A. CHART NO. 11429

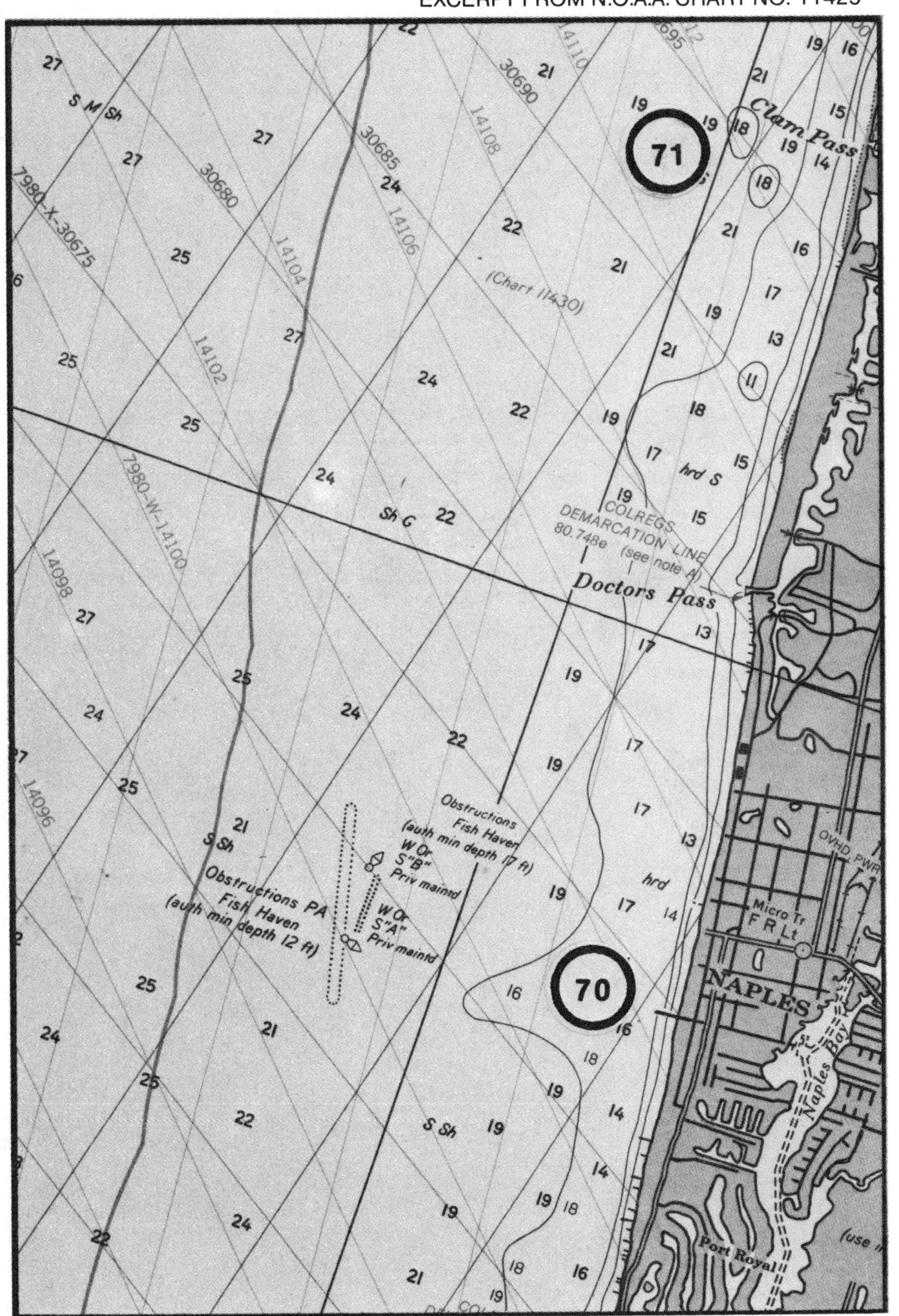

EXCERPT FROM N.O.A.A. CHART NO. 11427

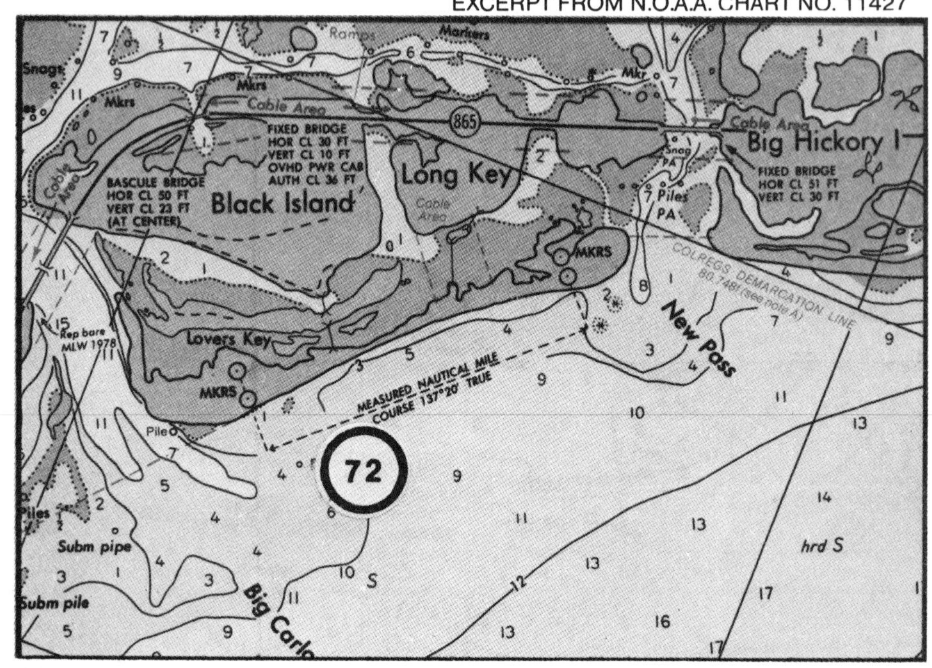

EXCERPT FROM N.O.A.A. CHART NO. 11427

EXCERPT FROM N.O.A.A. CHART NO. 11427

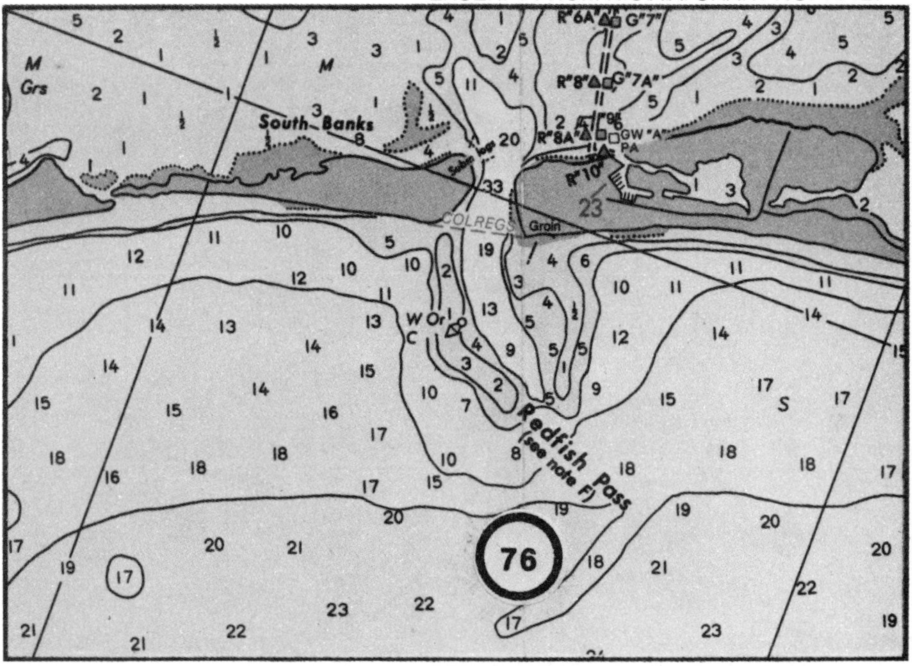

EXCERPT FROM N.O.A.A. CHART NO. 11427

EXCERPT FROM N.O.A.A. CHART NO. 11425

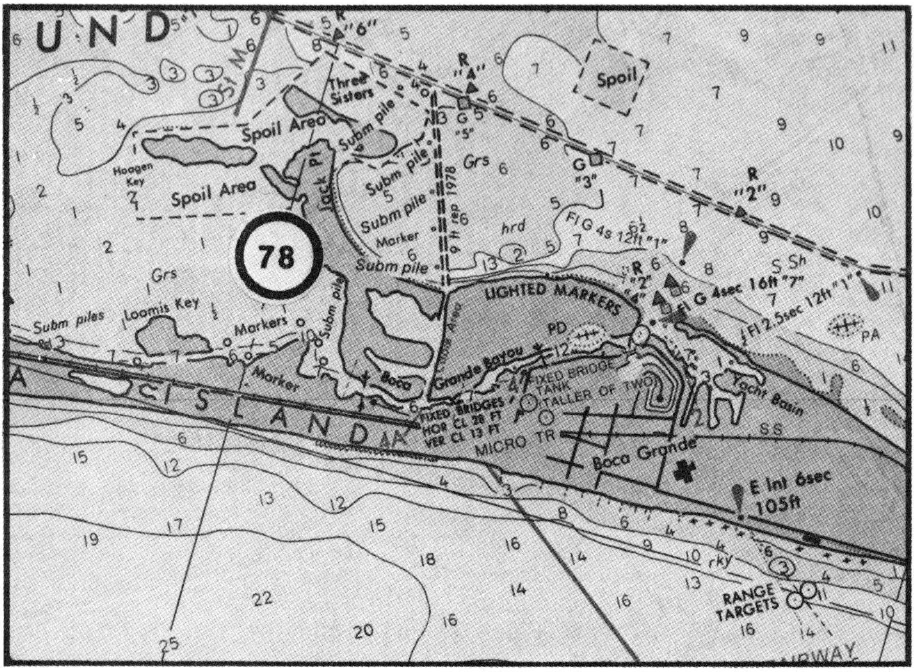

EXCERPT FROM N.O.A.A. CHART NO. 11425

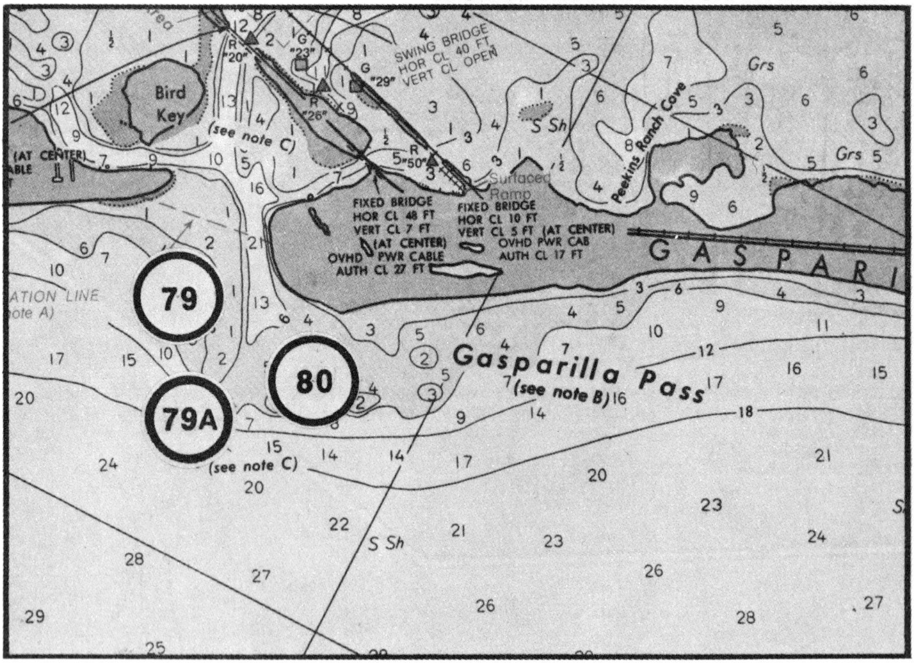

EXCERPT FROM N.O.A.A. CHART NO. 11425

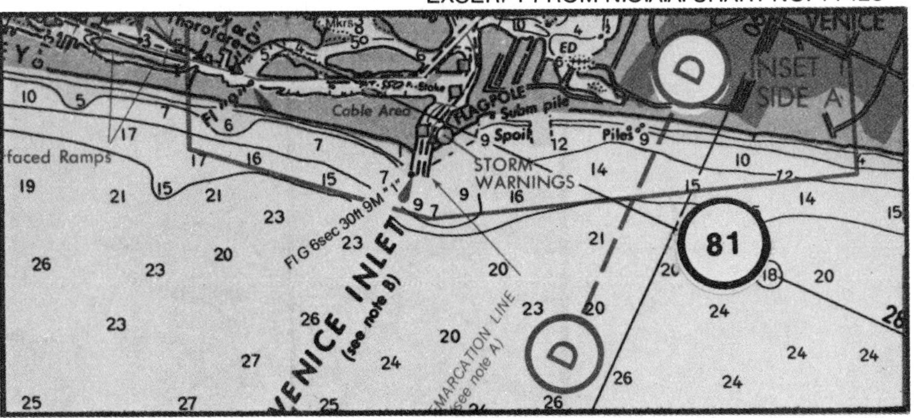

EXCERPT FROM N.O.A.A. CHART NO. 11425

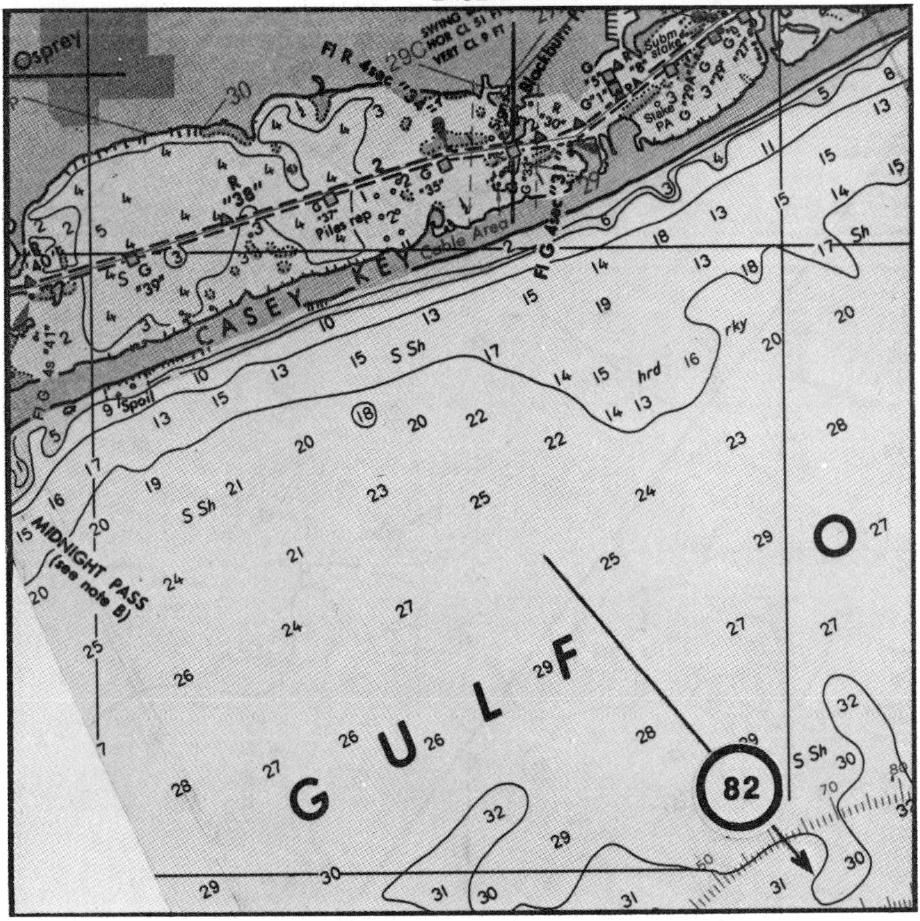

EXCERPT FROM N.O.A.A. CHART NO. 11424

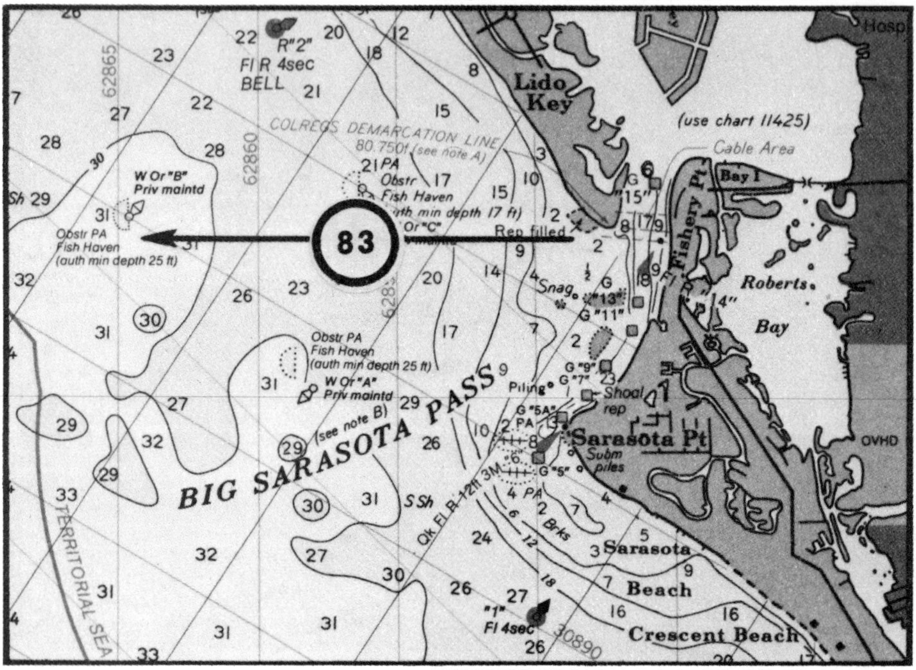

EXCERPT FROM N.O.A.A. CHART NO. 11425

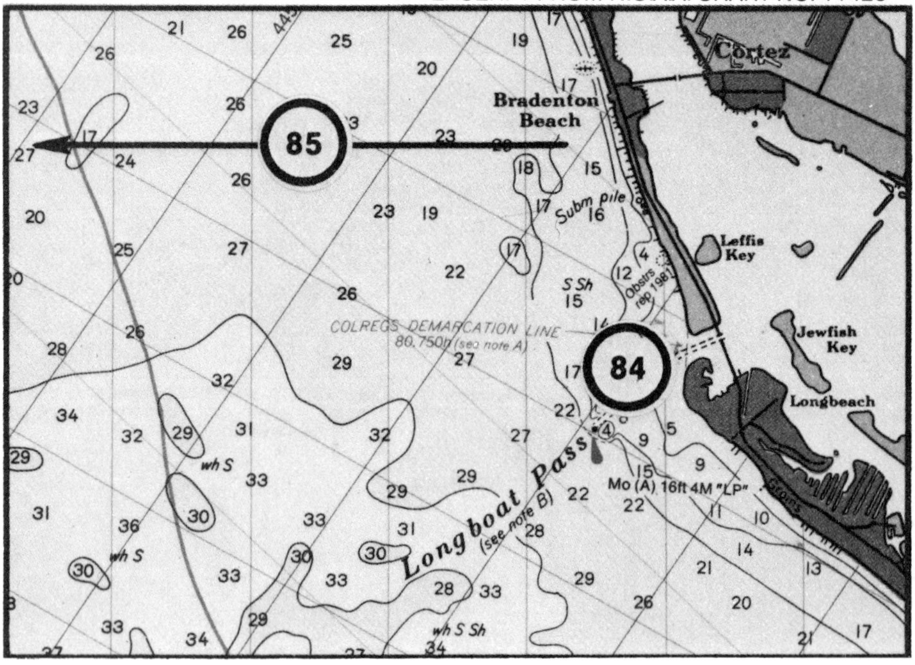

EXCERPT FROM N.O.A.A. CHART NO. 11424

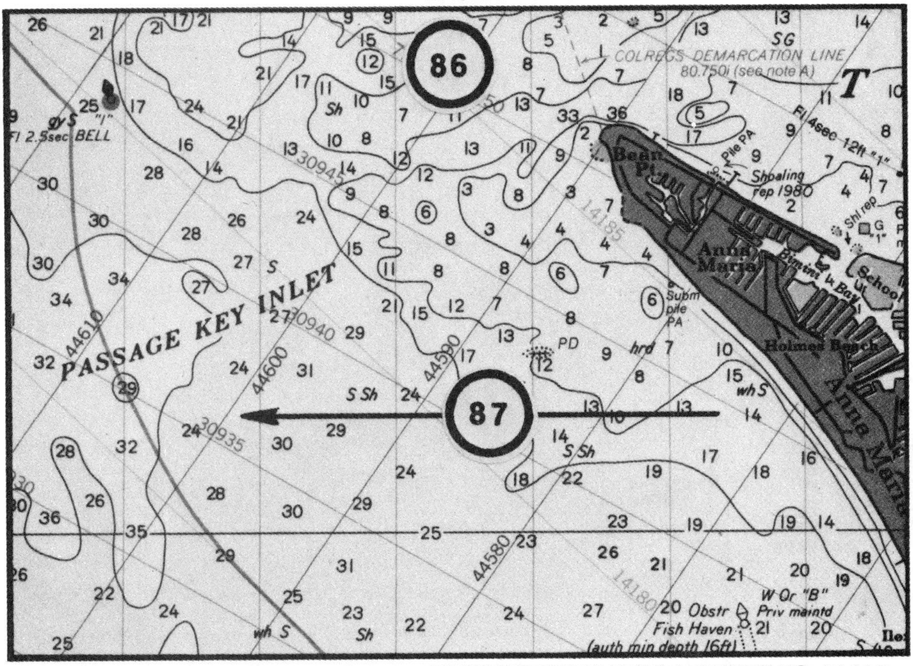

EXCERPT FROM N.O.A.A. CHART NO. 11412

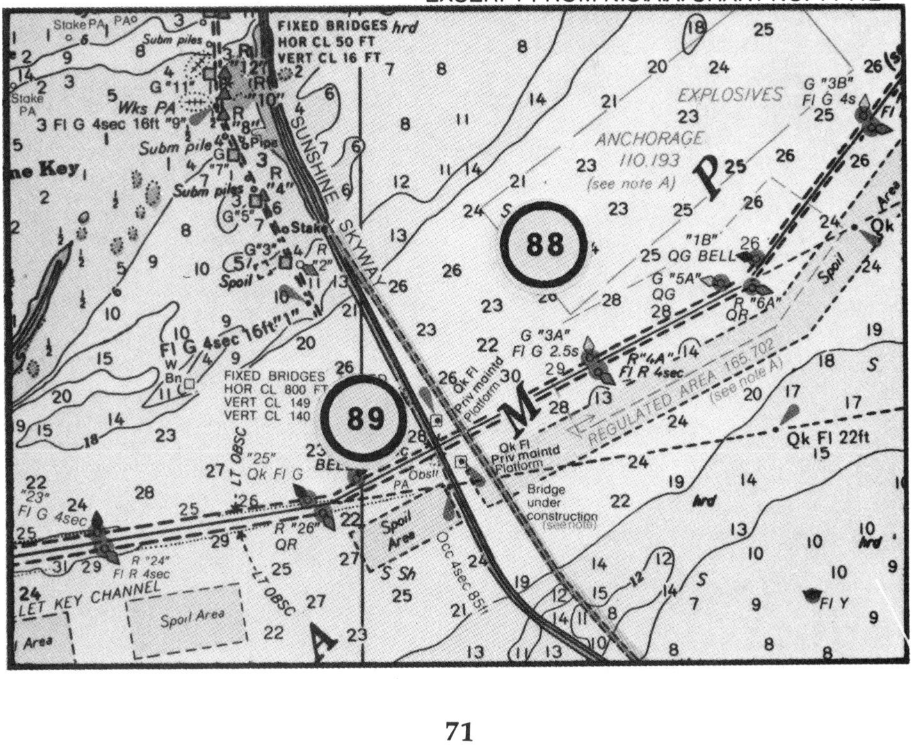

EXCERPT FROM N.O.A.A. CHART NO. 11412

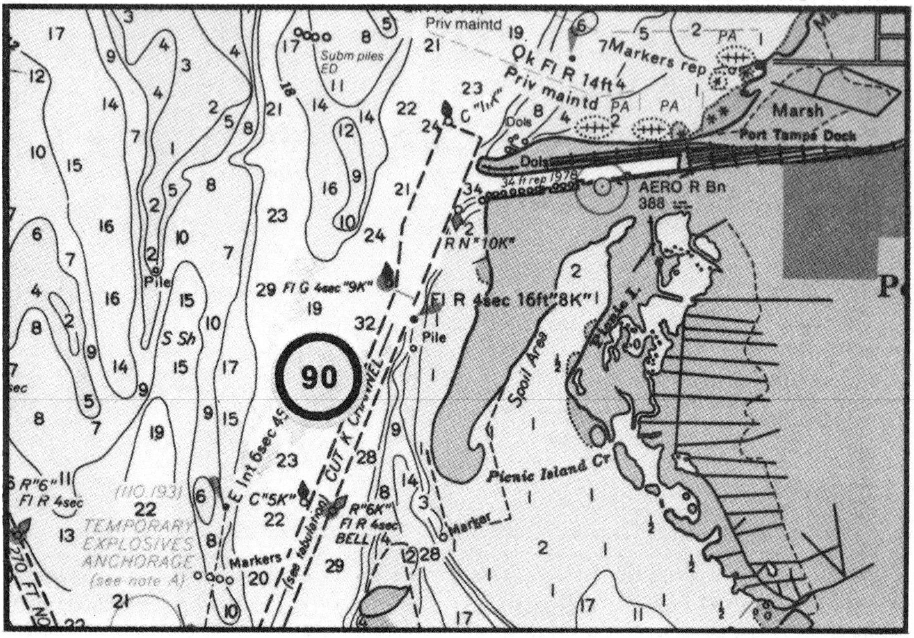

EXCERPT FROM N.O.A.A. CHART NO. 11412

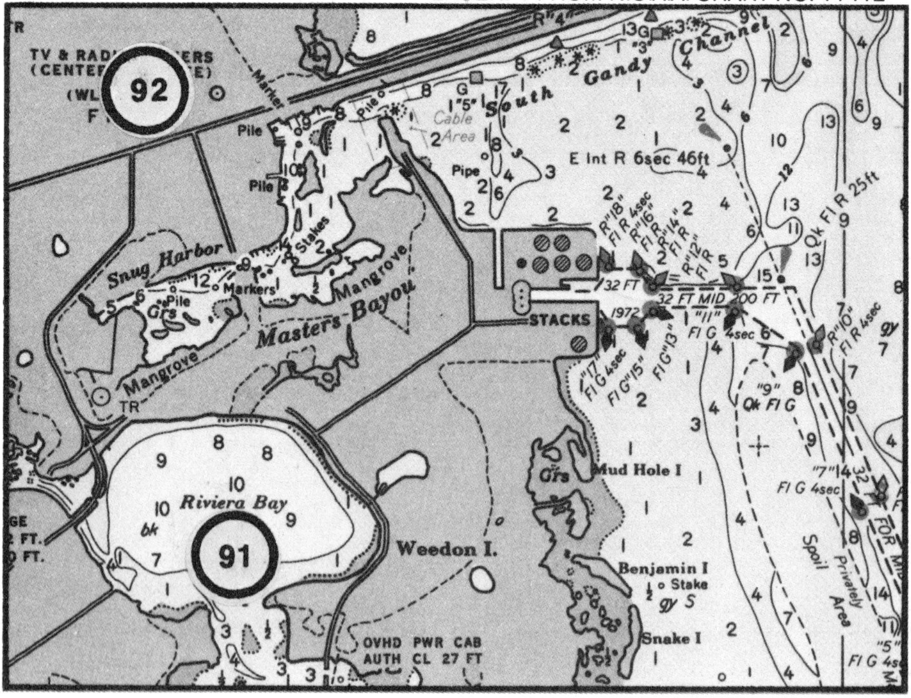

EXCERPT FROM N.O.A.A. CHART NO. 11413

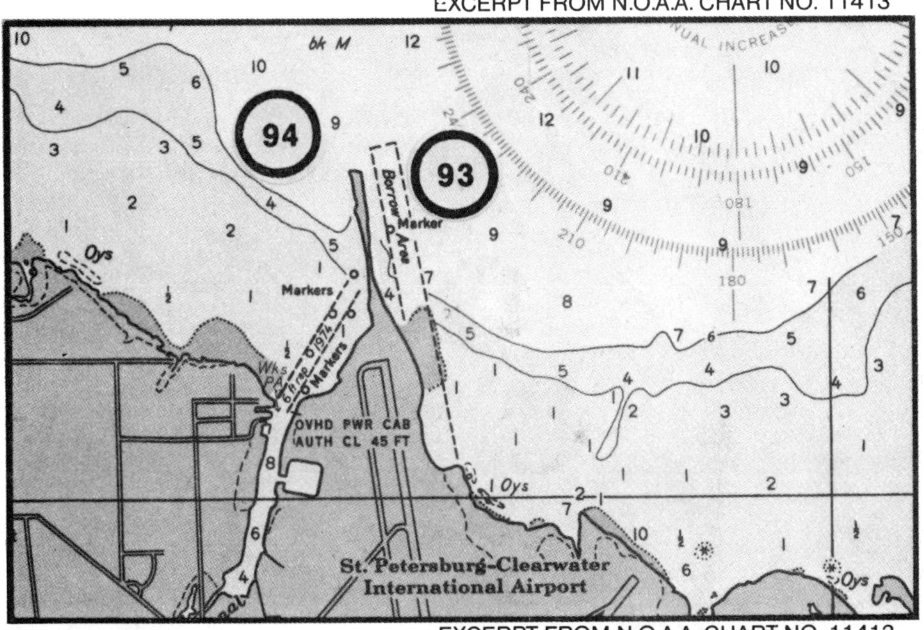

EXCERPT FROM N.O.A.A. CHART NO. 11413

Safety Harbor
Bishop Cr.
95
Mobbly Bayou
Mangrove
Pile
Philippe Pt.
OVERHEAD POWER CABLE
AUTHORIZED CL. 98 FT
STACK(W OF 3)
Booth Pt

EXCERPT FROM N.O.A.A. CHART NO. 11412

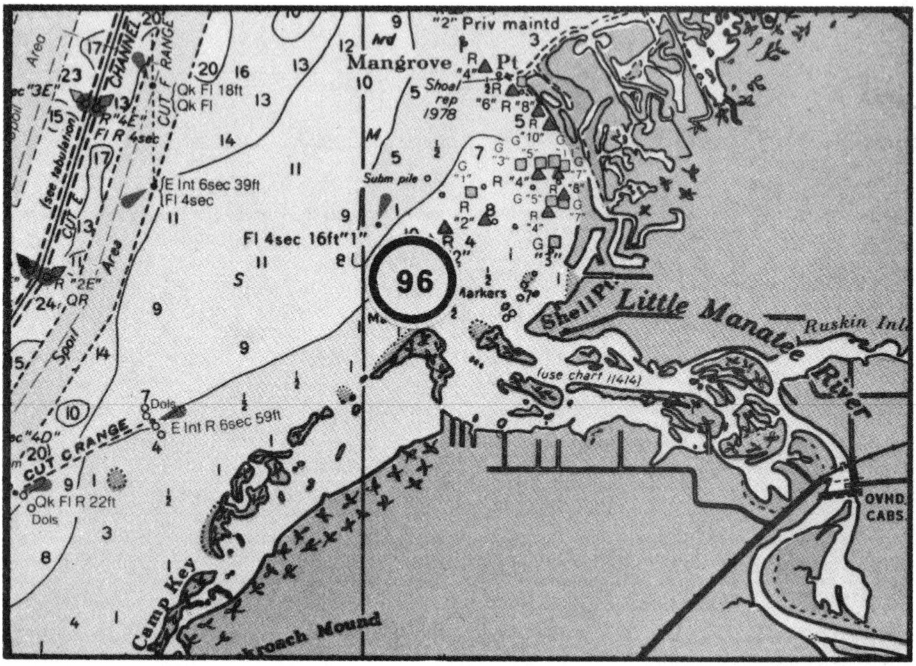

EXCERPT FROM N.O.A.A. CHART NO. 11412

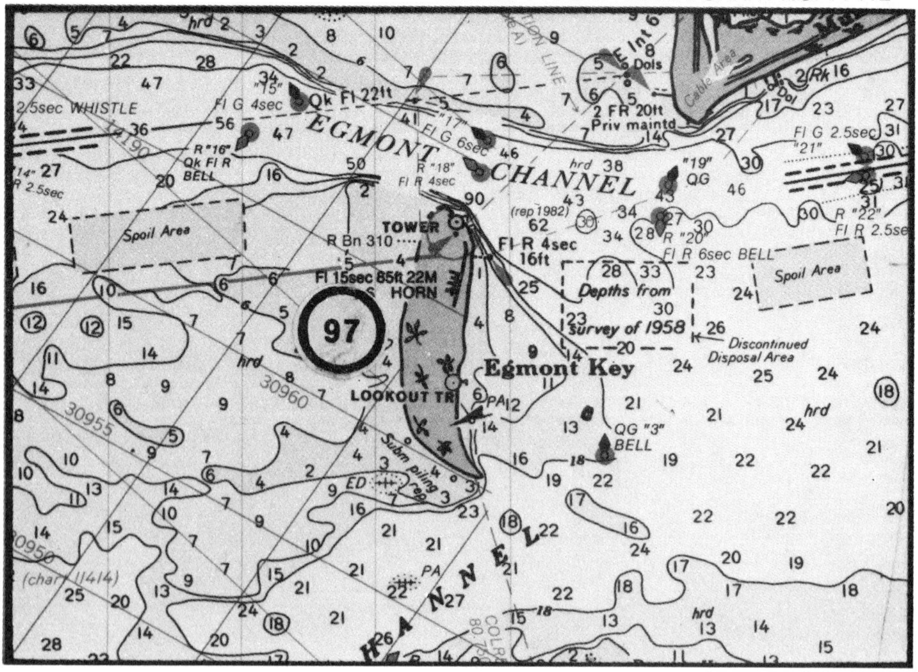

EXCERPT FROM N.O.A.A. CHART NO. 11412

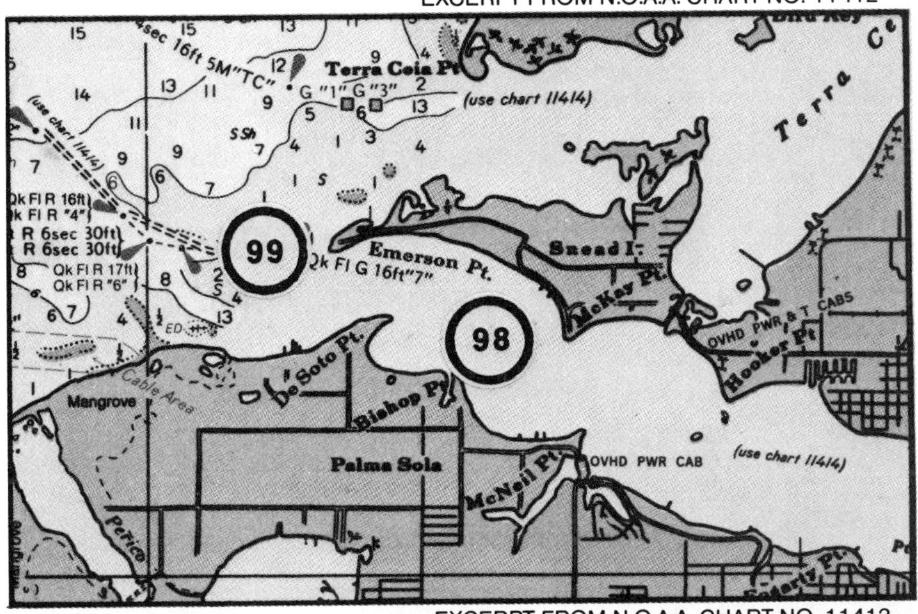

EXCERPT FROM N.O.A.A. CHART NO. 11413

EXCERPT FROM N.O.A.A. CHART NO. 11413

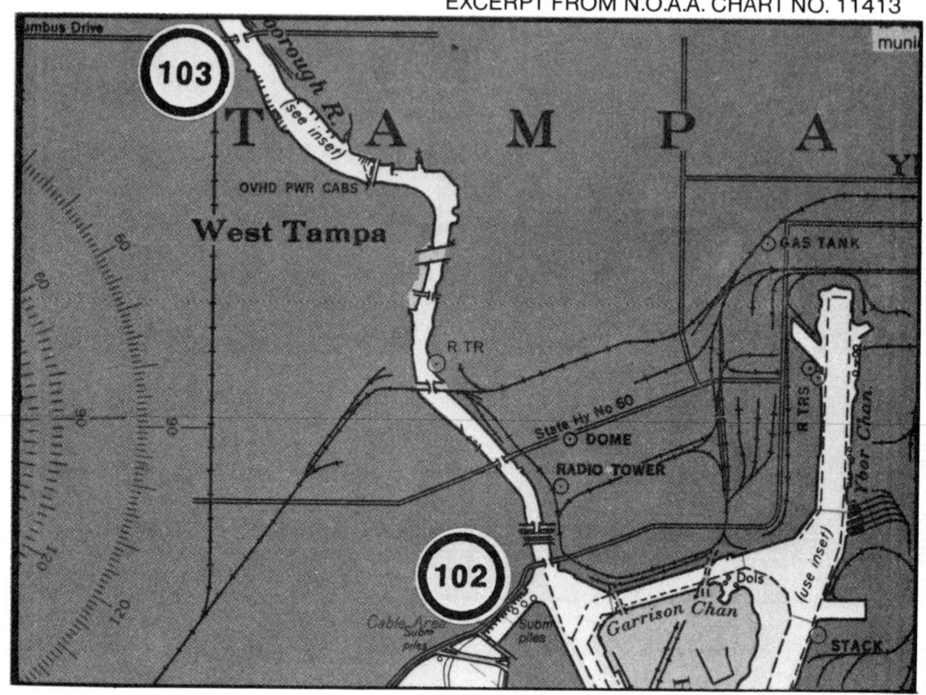

EXCERPT FROM N.O.A.A. CHART NO. 11413

Landing Lights
Mangrove
Coon Hammock Cr
104
Dol
PROHIBITED AREA (see note A) (204.100)
Air Force
105
hrd
Signs
E Int R 6sec 59ft
R "6"
R "4"

EXCERPT FROM N.O.A.A. CHART NO. 11409

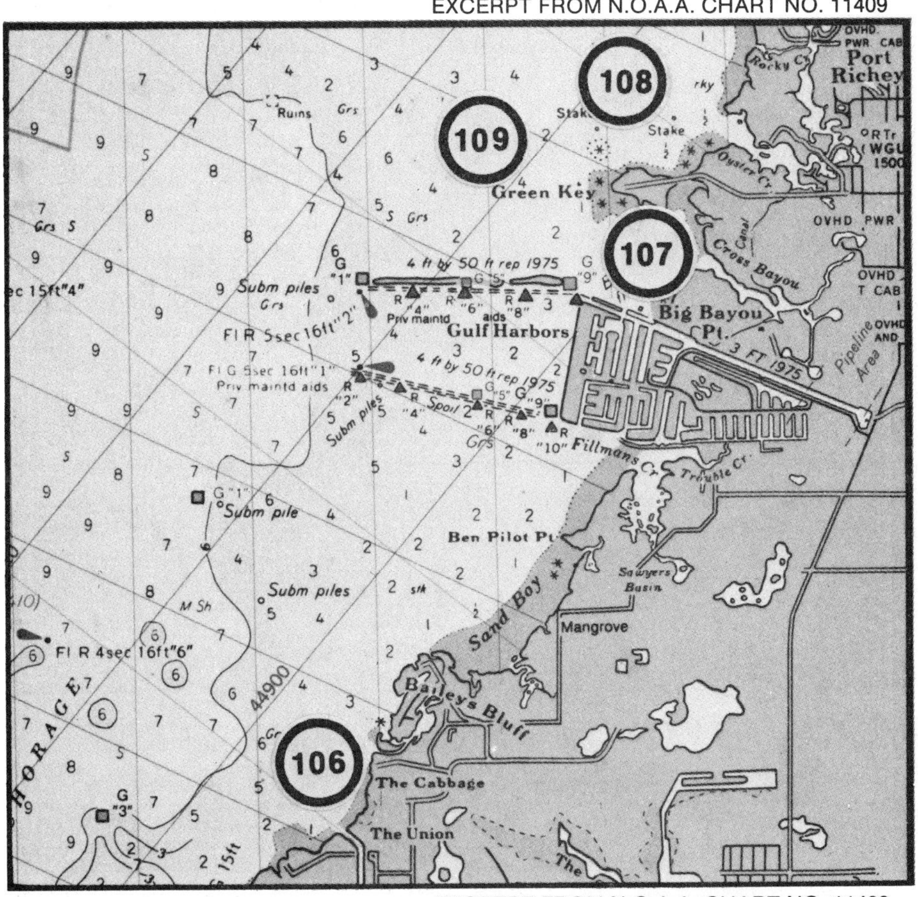

EXCERPT FROM N.O.A.A. CHART NO. 11409

EXCERPT FROM N.O.A.A. CHART NO. 11409

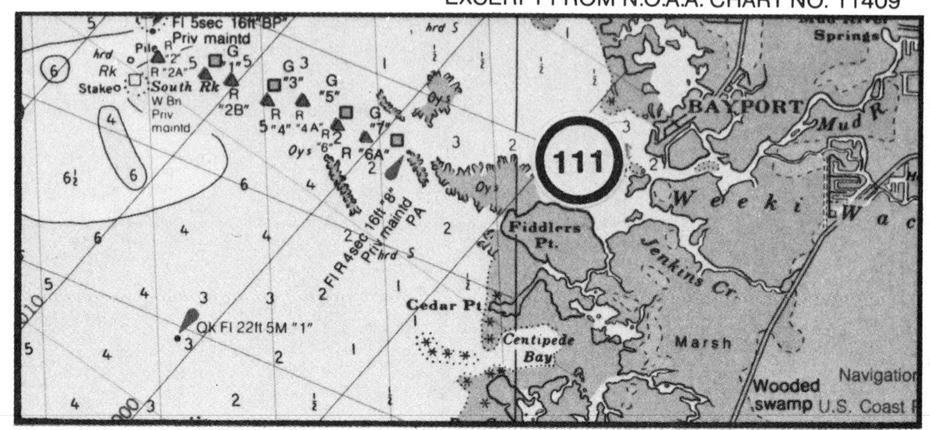

EXCERPT FROM N.O.A.A. CHART NO. 11409

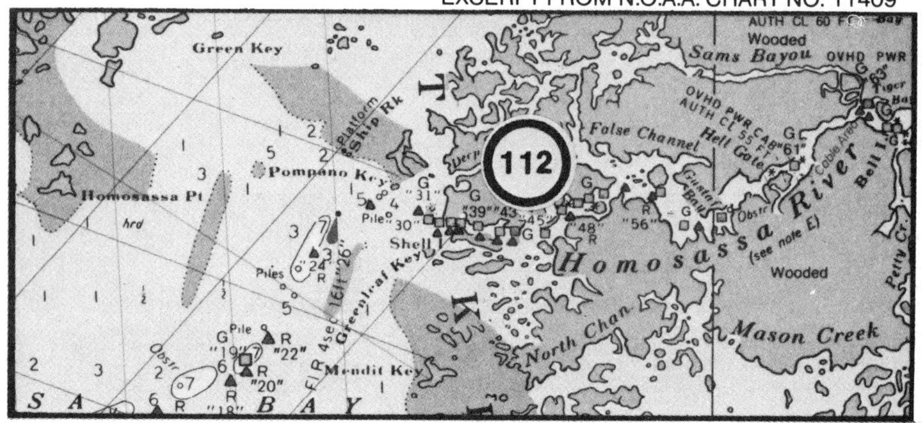

EXCERPT FROM N.O.A.A. CHART NO. 11408

EXCERPT FROM N.O.A.A. CHART NO. 11408

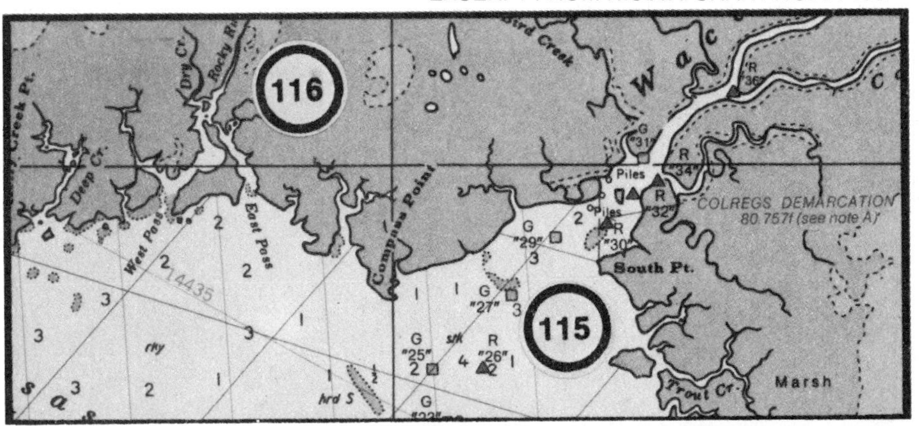

EXCERPT FROM N.O.A.A. CHART NO. 11408

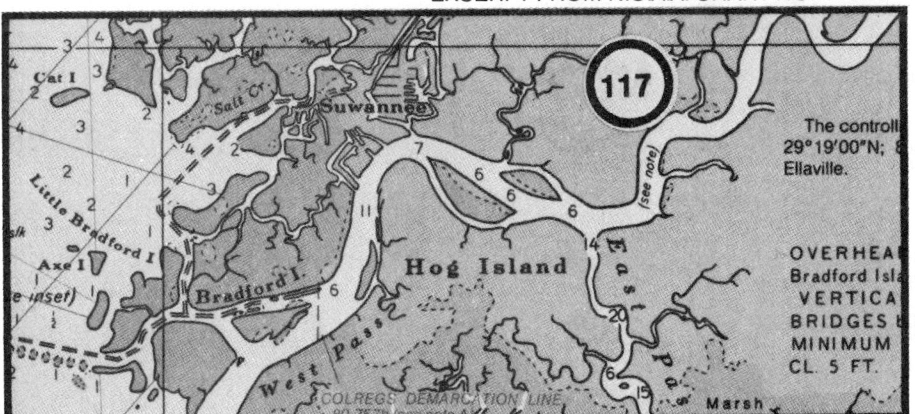

EXCERPT FROM N.O.A.A. CHART NO. 11407

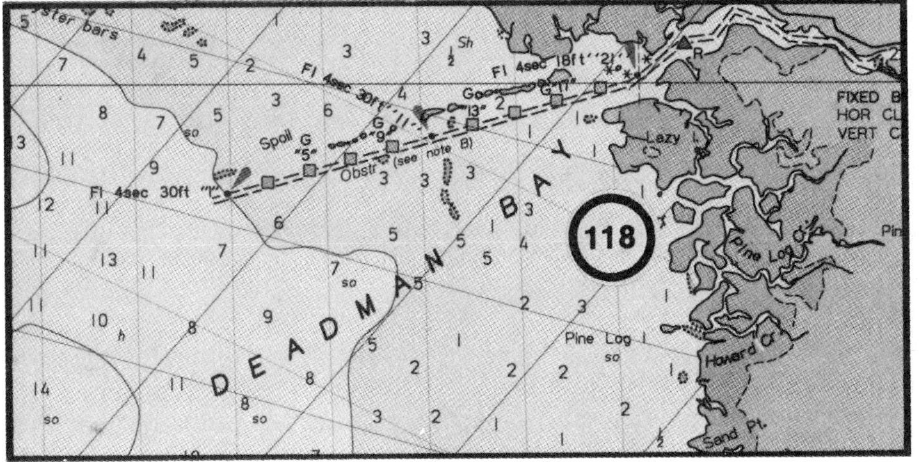

EXCERPT FROM N.O.A.A. CHART NO. 11405

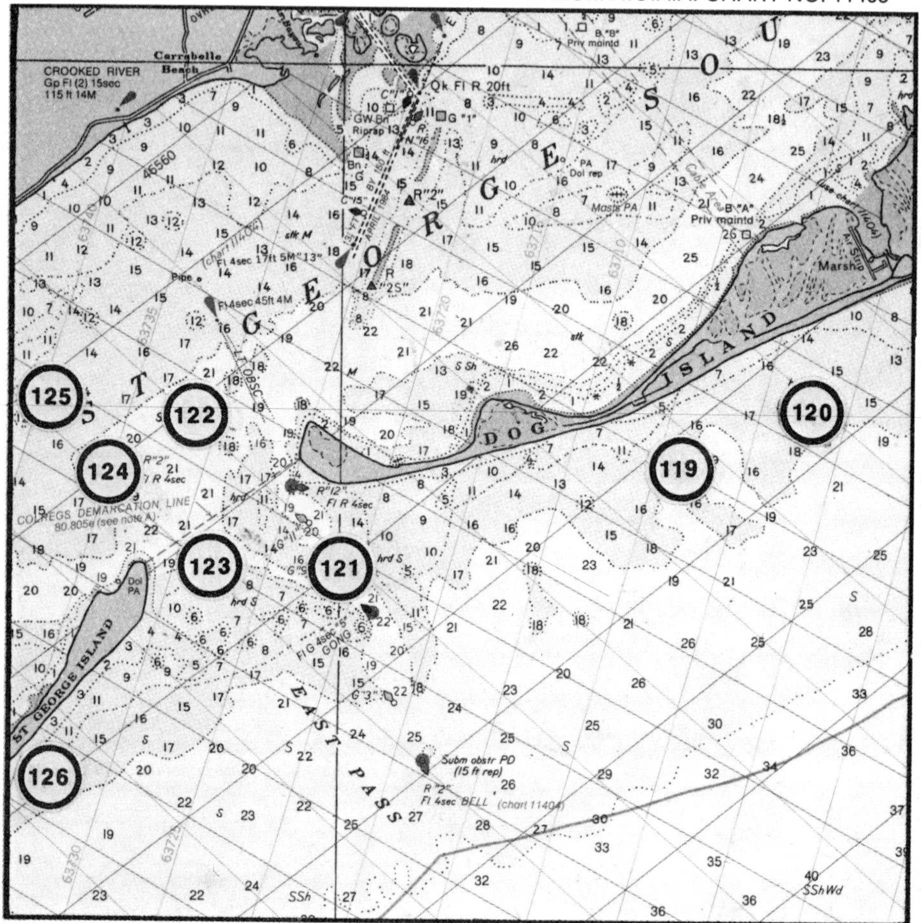

EXCERPT FROM N.O.A.A. CHART NO. 11401

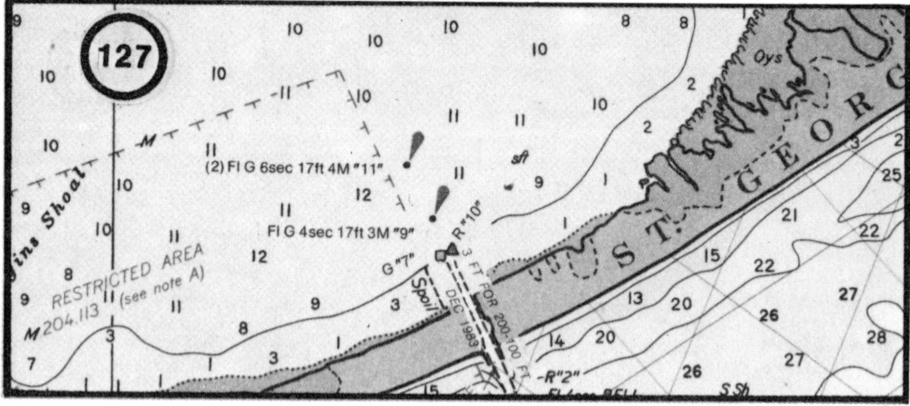

EXCERPT FROM N.O.A.A. CHART NO. 11401

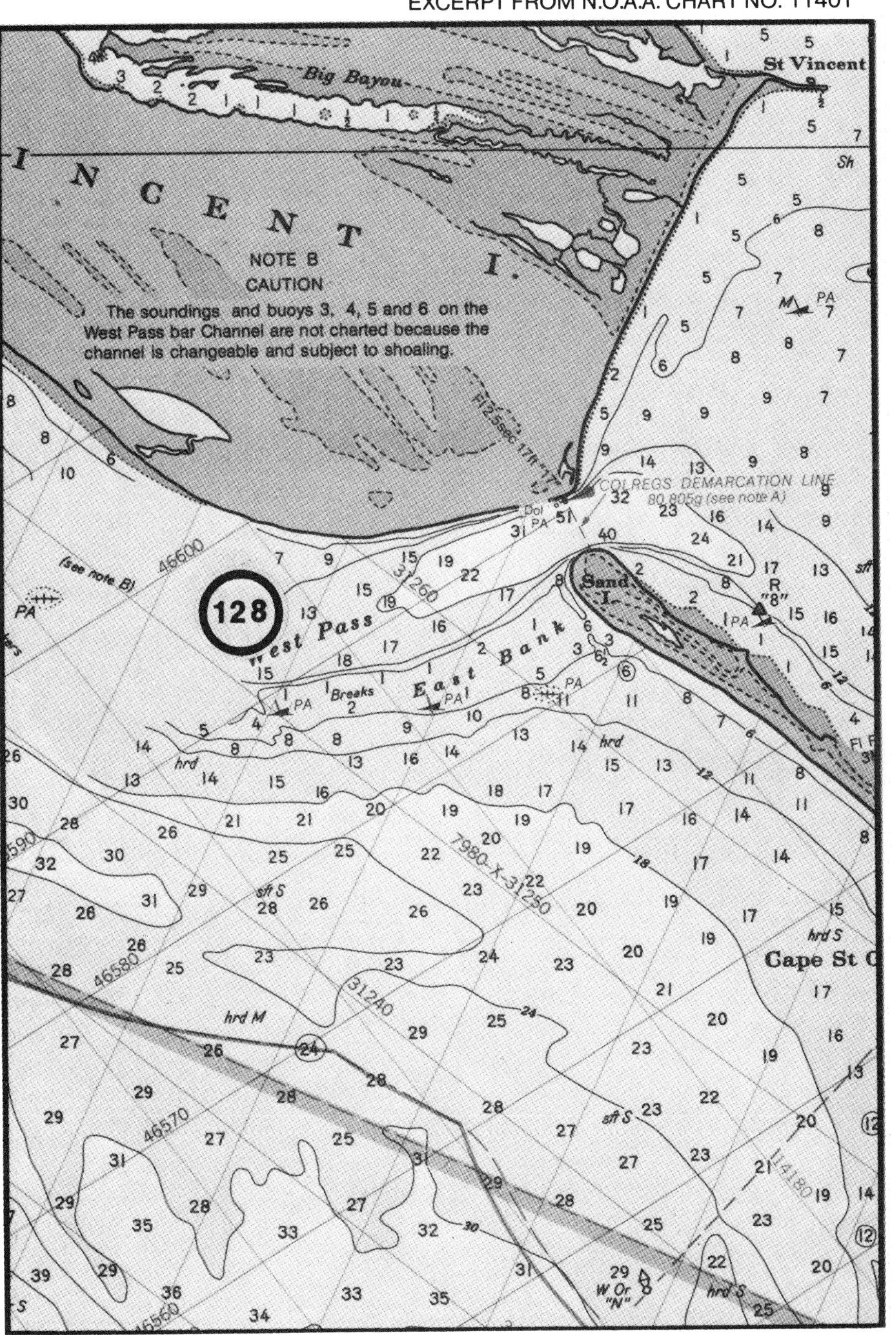

EXCERPT FROM N.O.A.A. CHART NO. 11382

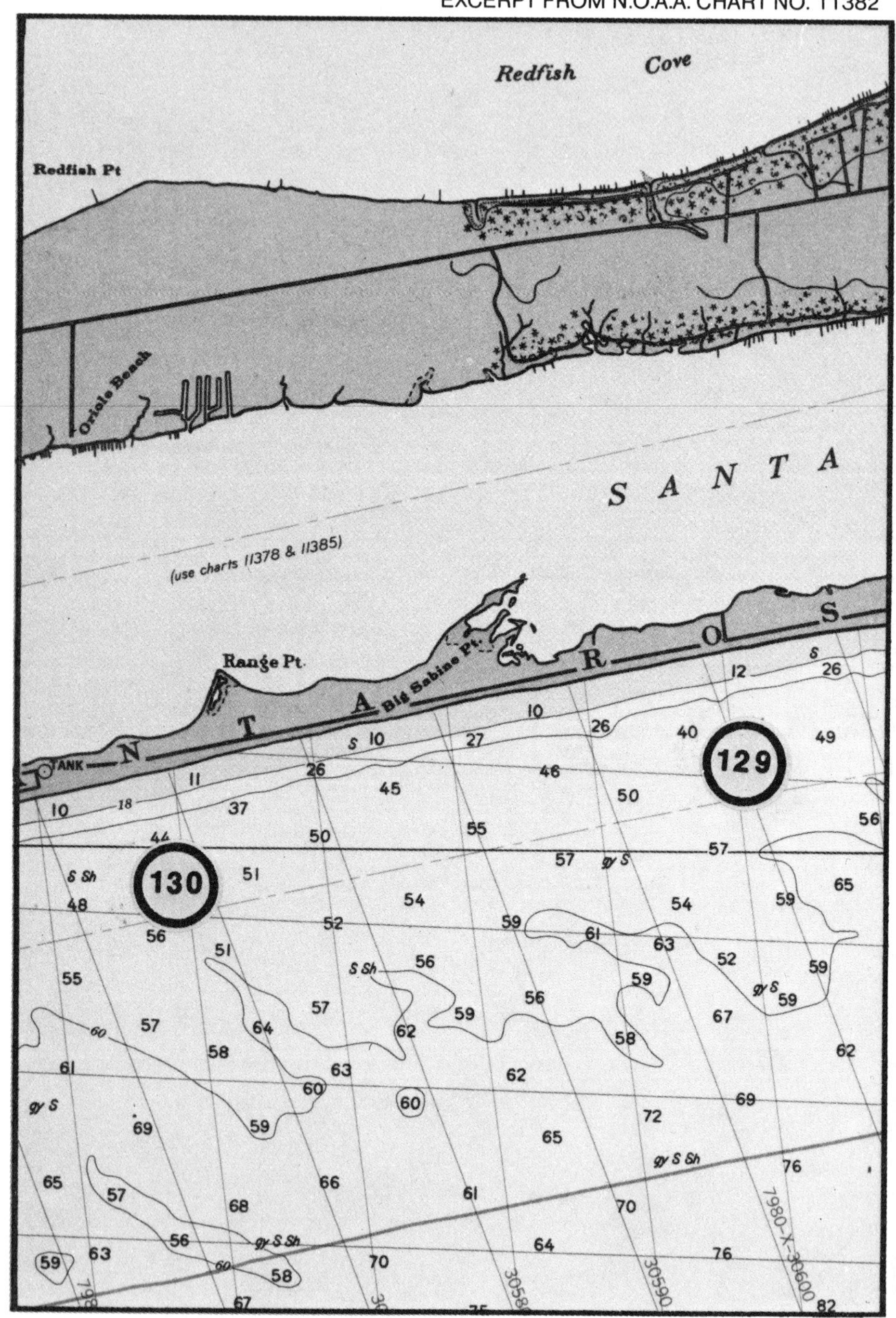

EXCERPT FROM N.O.A.A. CHART NO. 11389

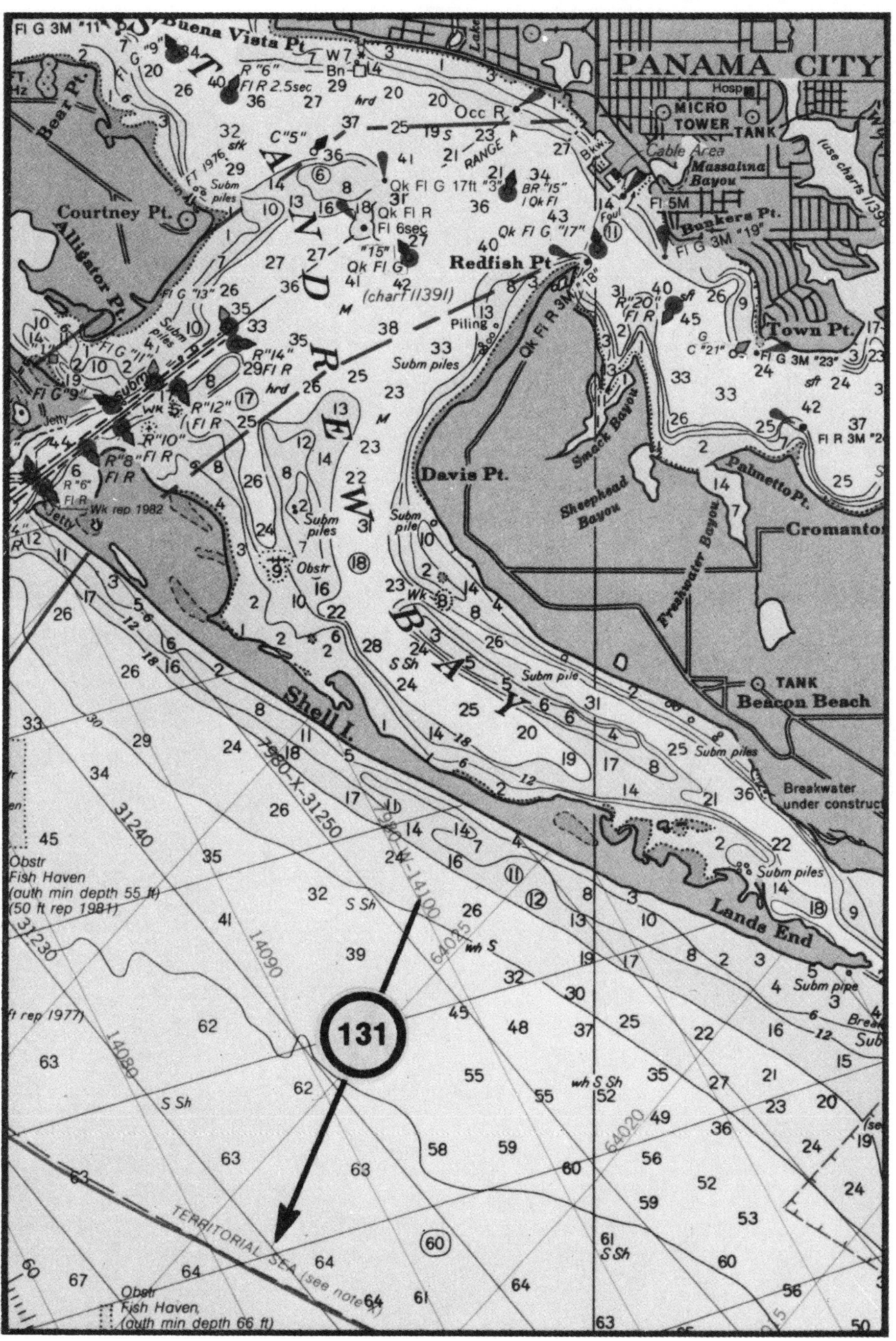

EXCERPT FROM N.O.A.A. CHART NO. 11382

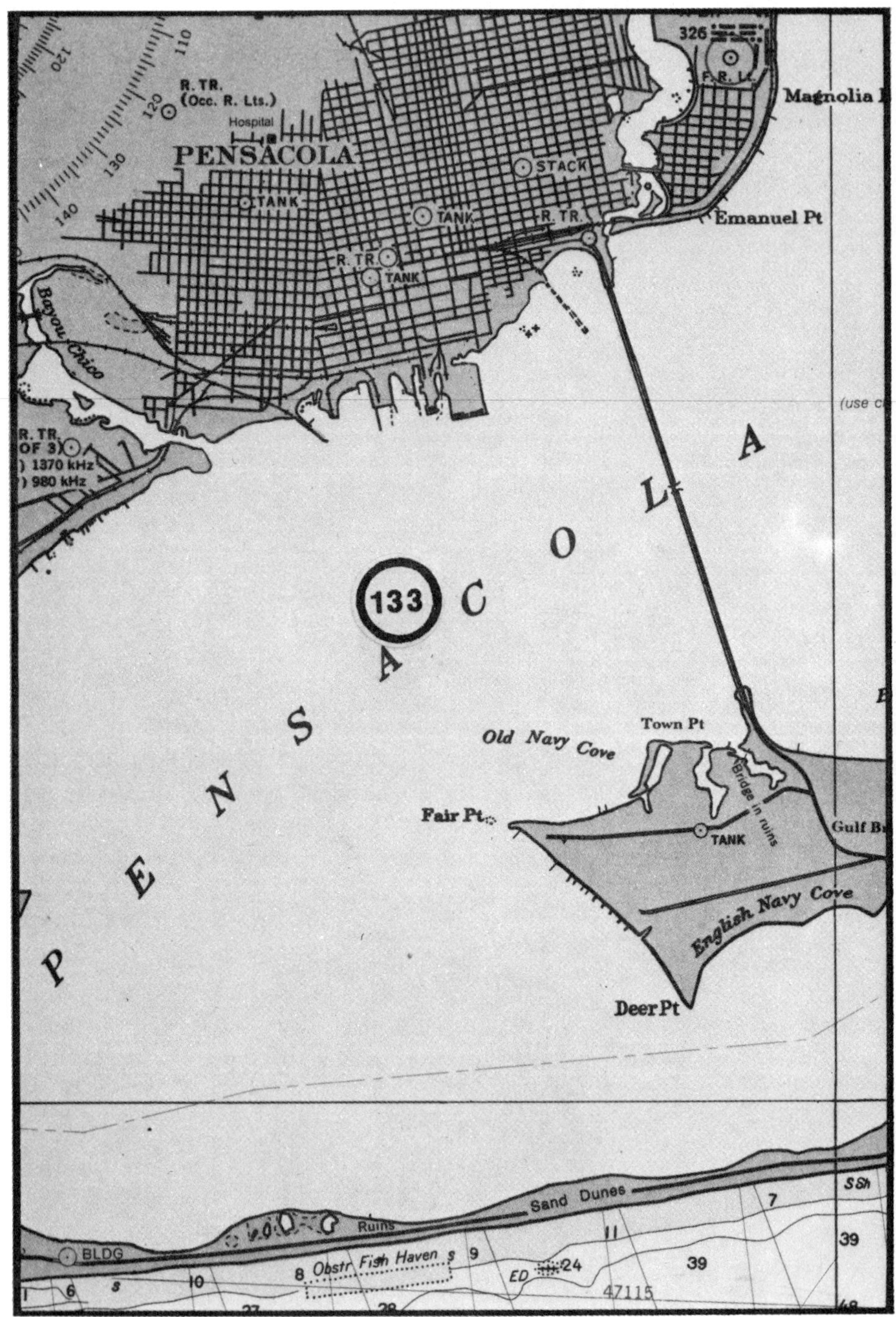

Basic Design Elements of Cob Coinage

Identifying and classifying the basic elements of design on Spanish cobs from the New World can be very helpful in shedding some light on the significant historical periods and transitions represented on this type of coinage.

There were two major types of designs on the obverse of Spanish cobs minted during this period. The first included a detail of the reigning monarch's shield; a basic version of the Hapsburg shield, with some variation from the reign of one king to another (or from mint to mint); the second replaced the monarch's shield with pillars, crossbars and waves, which later evolved into the well-known "pillar" dollar.

A study of the elements on the shield of the typical cob traces the lineage of the reigning royal families and kingdoms of this region of Europe, from which the various unified provinces later came to be known as Spain.

The typical Hapsburg shield, divided roughly into seven equal sections, featured alternating castle and lion figures appearing very prominently in the upper left-hand quadrant of the shield, symbolic of the two original medieval kingdoms of Leon (lion) and Castilla (castle). Aragon, represented by the vertical lines or stripes, was joined to Castile and Leon by the marriage of Ferdinand of Aragon to Isabel of Castile, who subsequently conquered Granada in 1492. The pomegranate symbol of Granada frequently appears next to the lion/castle arrangement. Naples and Sicily, at one time under the control of Spain, are represented by the eagle symbols in the upper right hand corner.

Moving to the center, the solid horizontal bar on the left (below the lions and castles) is representational of Austria, which with the (Tirolean) eagle had long been a major part of the coat-of-arms of the House of Hapsburg. The Fleur-de-lis, evidently representational of France (the house of Burgundy and the French Bourbons), is also a recurrent theme, variations of which are usually represented in the right hand center of the shield.

At the bottom left hand side of the shield are the diagonal (and later curved) stripes or lines of Old Burgundy. On the lower center, and lower right hand respectively, are the lions of Flanders and Brabant, coming under Spanish rule with Charles I.

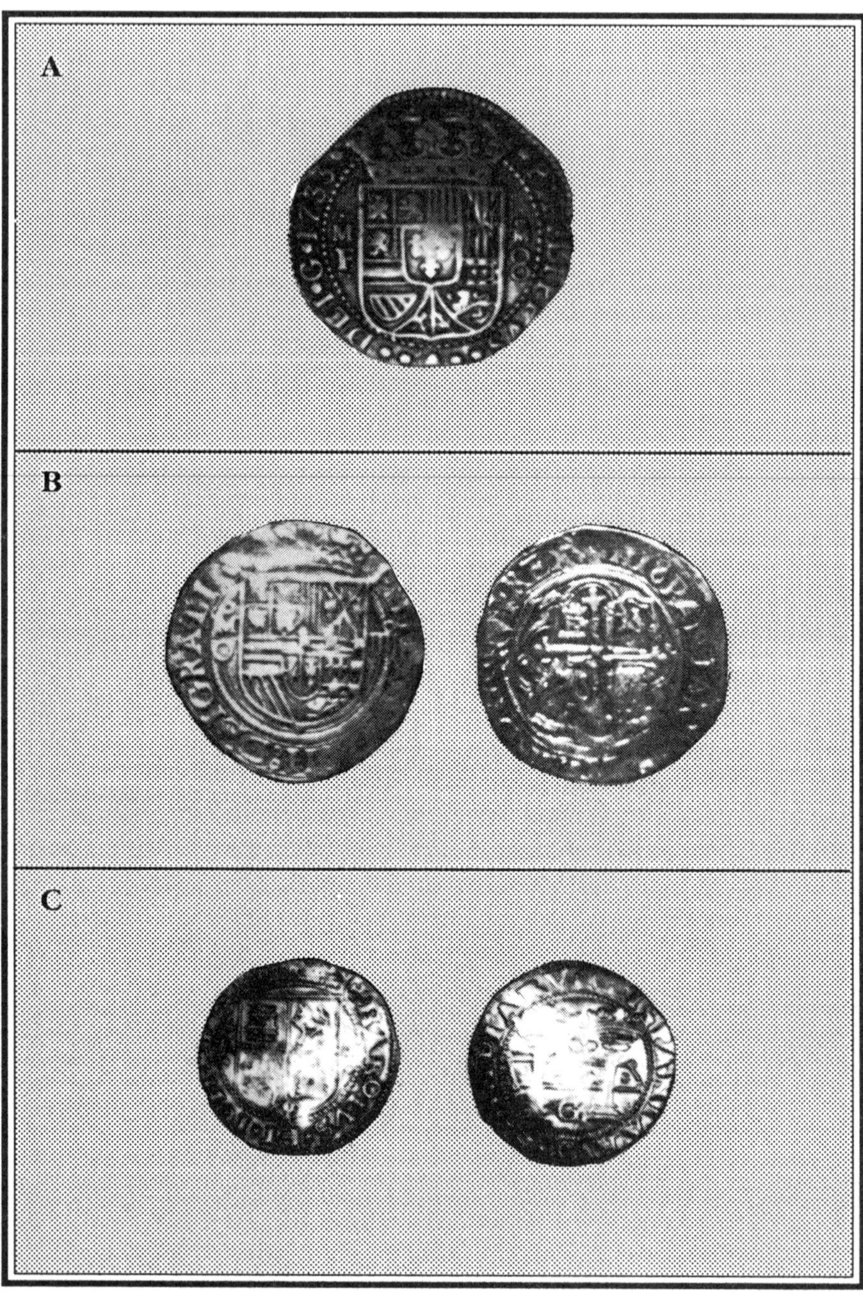

A. 8 reales, Mexico, 1733 MF
B. 4 reales, Mexico, Philip II, Assayer O
C. 2 reales, Mexico, Assayer G

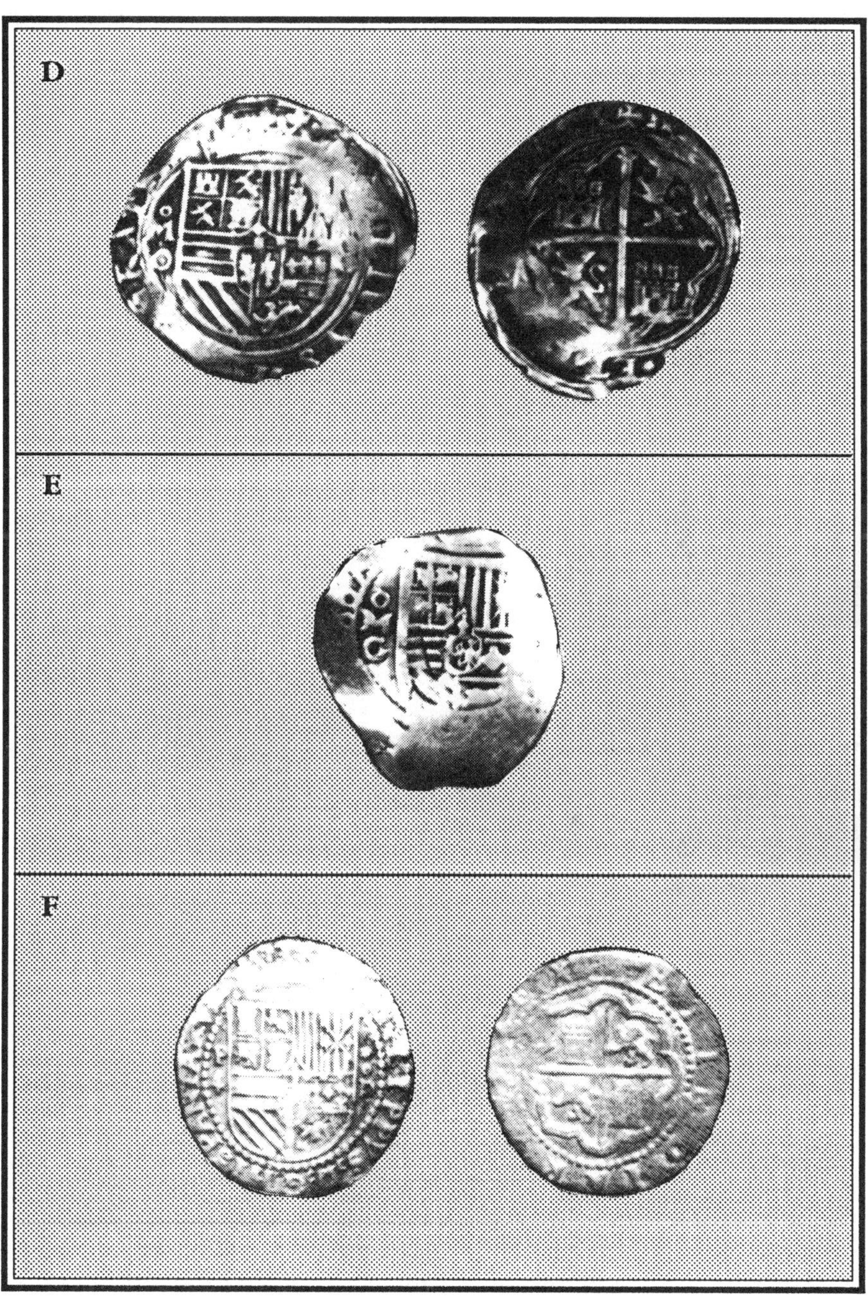

D. 8 reales, Philip II, Assayer O

E. 4 reales, Mexico, 1609

F. 4 reales, Lima, Assayer Diego de la Torre

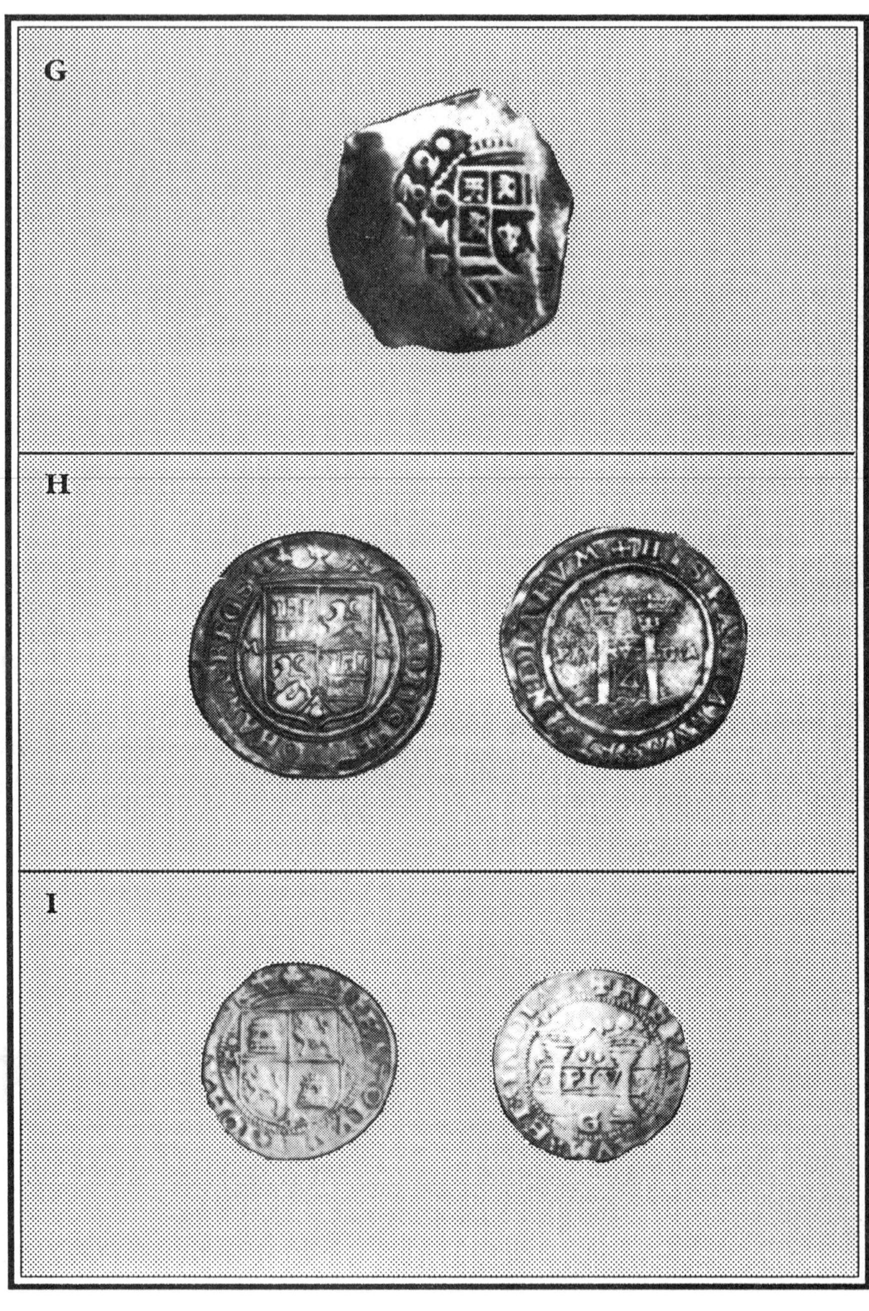

G. 8 reales, Mexico, 1732

H. 4 reales, Mexico, Assayer G (M-G)

I. 2 reales, Mexico, Carlos-Juana, Assayer G, Early series

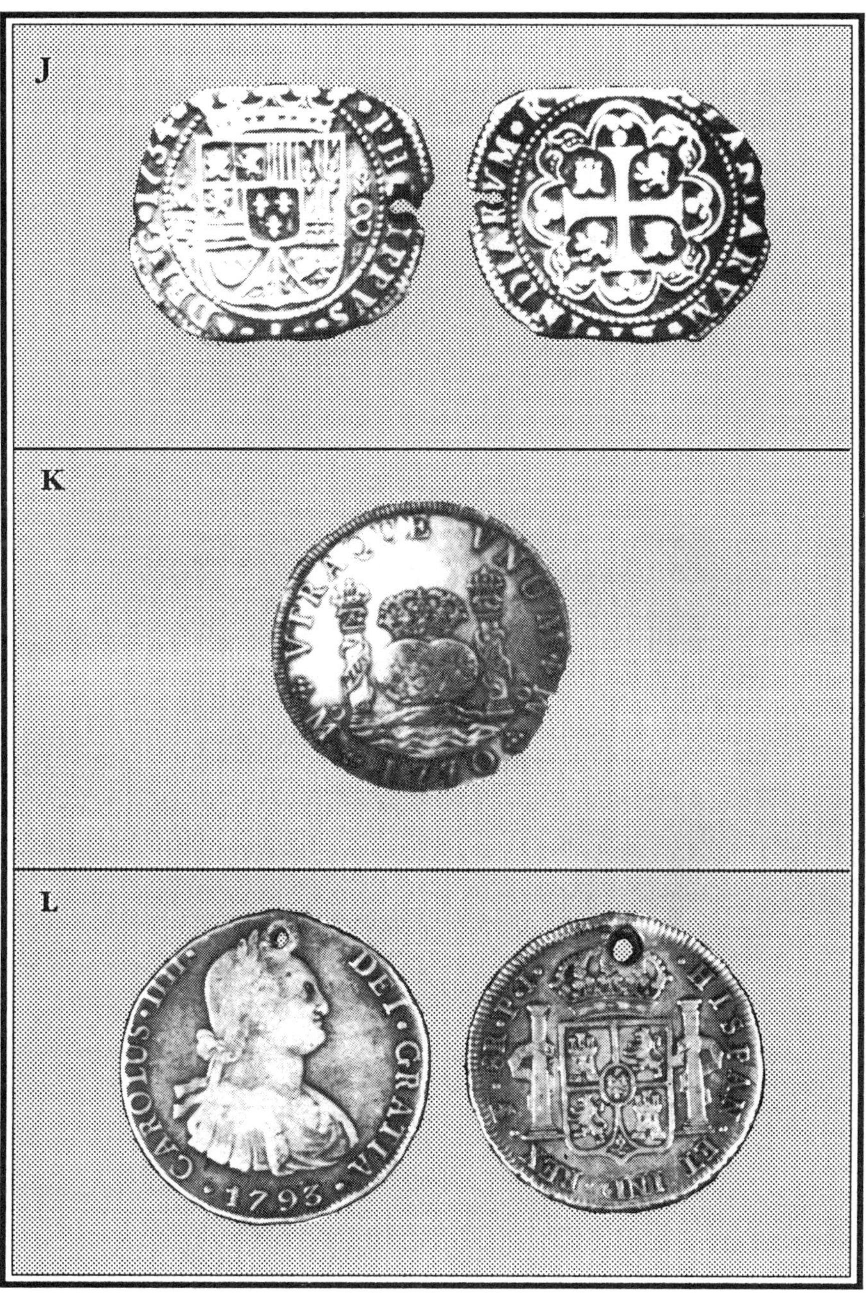

J. 8 reales, Mexico, 1734 MF, transition coinage
K. 8 reales, Pillar dollar, 1770
L. Pillar dollar, 1793